Pollokshaws Through Time

George Rountree

Looking north from near the Factory Street bridge in 1896, this tranquil semi-rural/industrial scene by the River Cart was taken from where Auldhouse Park would be laid out in the 1920s. In the area where the entrance to Brown & Adam's works would be, to the left of the small building close to the riverbank, there is what looks like a small thatched building or a tarpaulin covered haystack. The chimney of the gas works coking plant is in the centre, while the one to the right carried away the smoke and fumes from the forge of the engineering works of Stewart & McKenzie's in what was then Factory Street. The Townshouse tower can just be made out behind a tree in the dip to the left of the gas works chimney.

© 2009 George Rountree
First Published in the United Kingdom, 2010
Stenlake Publishing Limited
54-58 Mill Square, Catrine, KA5 6RD
www.stenlake.co.uk

ISBN 9781840334852

Acknowledgements

Thanks to Pollokshaws Heritage for allowing me to ransack their collection of around 500 photos for the best prints, and the many people who contributed to it over the past 25 years - in particular Nettie Wren, who took a number of the photographs included here.

The following photographs are reproduced by courtesy of the Mitchell Library, Glasgow City Council: front cover, pages 2 (upper), 10 (lower), 24 (upper), 27 (both), 33 (upper), 36 (upper), 41 (lower), 49 (upper), 51 (lower), 57 (upper), 59 (both), 60 (lower), 61 (both), 65 (both), 67 (upper), 68 (upper), 72 (both), 73 (lower right), 74 (upper), 76 (lower), 77 (both), 78 (both), 79 (both), 80 (upper), 84 (both), 85 (upper), 86 (both), 89 (upper), 90 (both), 92 (both), 93 (upper), and inside back cover.

Baird's Bridge, Factory Street, 1922. The tenement of two closes, 36 and 42 Factory Street, was probably built more than 20 years before this time. Note the shadow of Brown & Adams' boiler house chimney on the nearer face, and the upper part of an office block and gatehouse at the factory entrance on the left showing above the fence. There was a pub in the low building to the right of the tenement which stood at the corner of Kirk Lane.

Prototype experimental tram 1142, pictured in the late 1950s at the by then seldom-used terminus at Nether Auldhouse Road. It was likely to have been on a Scottish Tramways Museum Society's member's special. In an arrangement with the Tramways Department, the STMS ran occasional trips for members as the system contracted. As sections of track became disused it was their aim to travel along them one last time before the power supply was switched off and the rails lifted. Harriet Street corner is visible on the left beyond the tram, and the Shawholm Street nameplate is just showing on the right, close to the tram's rear vision mirror. Tram drivers had to take care not to run off the end of the track and lose contact with the power supply!

Introduction

Two domestic scenes from the 1930s . . .

Kitchen windows in tenements built between 1890 and 1920 were usually a single casement 3' 3" wide. As the outer walls of the buildings were more than two feet thick, the windows were recessed on the inside by about eighteen inches, and had a sill on the outside of about eight inches. A standard original fitting in the sides of the recess, which were angled at about thirty degrees opening out into the kitchen, were shutters 20 inches in width reaching up to the full window height, and hinged at the outer edge next to it. They were panelled and like the other woodwork were painted brown. The shutters could be closed to cover the window, although they seem to have fallen out of use by the 1930s.

The window recess housed two of the main items of equipment in the kitchen, the sink and worktop. The white-glazed pottery sink, referred to by older people as 'the jawbox', was boxed in with wood panelling to form cupboards which stretched across the full width in front of the recess and a little beyond on both sides. Other older tenements had sinks of blackened cast iron that could never be made to look clean. Above the cupboards and alongside the sink, the worktop was an inch-thick solid piece of wood, fitted level so that it didn't drain. A single swan-neck water tap was a standard fitting in all houses in working class areas. It was called a 'crane', and was fitted on one side above the sink on a low bulkhead at the foot of the casement shutter. This provided a low shelf to hold items like a soap dish, nail and tooth brushes, shaving equipment, pumice stones, scrubbing brushes, and steel wool for cleaning the iron cooking pots. The 'crane', the upper part of which stood above the level of this shelf, could be turned down into the sink to enable the shutter on that side to be closed, or to allow another board to be placed over the sink to give extra workspace if required. Only now, more than 70 years on, do I realise why the tap was called a 'crane'; it was because it could be made to 'luff' like the jib of a crane.

One of my earliest memories is sitting on the worktop, aged around three, with my feet in a basin of water, being washed before going to bed in the dark of a winter evening. Quite clear is the recollection of looking out past the side of the blind into the dim gas-lit street and seeing the many illuminated windows of the houses in the building opposite. Domestic gaslights were housed on the walls rather than the ceilings, and at this time all windows had blinds of beige paper or fabric. This meant that the silhouette of anyone working at their sink or drainer was projected onto the blind, making them visible from outside. Frequent movements were to be seen of people busy with one of the never-ending household chores like preparing a meal, washing dishes, a man just in from work stropping an open razor then shaving and washing himself, or a woman doing a washing and using a scrubbing board. In those days domestic chores took up far more time than they do today. 'Love's Old Sweet Song' was a popular favourite on the wireless at that time and the words are indelibly printed on my memory: 'Just a song at twilight/ When the lights are low/ As the flickering shadows/ Softly come and go'. They appeared to my very young perception to have been specially made up to describe that vision for me. It was the first of many occasions when, for me, a piece of music has become associated with an event or an experience.

Firewood for lighting fires could be bought as ready to use bunches of sticks from hardware stores, ironmonger's, newsagent's, larger grocery stores, and street traders. They were usually made from old railway sleepers which, having been treated with creosote, burned well. The sticks were cut to a convenient size, about eight inches long, not too thick or they wouldn't catch alight, or too thin as they would be consumed too quickly before the cinders, recovered from the previous day's fire and laid on top, could start burning. A bunch held as many sticks as could be grasped in a loop a little larger than would be made between the hands with middle fingers and thumbs almost touching, and were tied with a length of twine which incorporated a carrying loop. In the 1930s they cost three halfpence a bunch, but I remember selling them when I worked in the Co-op grocers in the 1940s and '50s, by which time they cost tuppence ha'ppeny, or 1p in today's money.

It was seldom necessary to buy sticks for our household because my Dad, an engineer, brought home pieces of wood from his work. Engineering works handling heavy materials always had baulks of timber lying about for use as props and chocks. The smaller pieces, which had become covered with oil and grease, were carried off home by workers to be used as kindling. A local street trader used to sell bags of ordinary box and other scrap wood from his horsedrawn cart, and once or twice when Dad's supply failed to turn up a much-criticised bridging quantity lacking the oil contaminant was bought from him.

The wood brought home by Dad was sawn across the grain into eight-inch thick sections. He took them out to the landing and there, kneeling on the doormat and working over the doorstep and using a small axe, he would split the sections down to the required size. This job, done weekly in winter, was somehow always tackled on a Friday evening and fascinated me as I could not wait to be old enough to be allowed to use the axe. Landing surfaces in front of house doors in tenements were invariably chipped by the axe, but the marks were covered up when the doormat was replaced. People living in these houses today where the surface of the landing is as it was originally may well wonder how the marks came to be made. My job in this operation was to gather up the chopped sticks and place them properly aligned and tidy in the storage box, a wooden New Zealand 56 lb. bulk butter box scrounged from the Co-op. At this point a childhood rhyme comes to mind: One two, buckle my shoe,/ Three four open the door,/ Five six break up sticks,/ Seven eight lay them straight,/ Nine ten a big fat hen'.

That seemingly irrelevant last line was probably intended as an expression of relief at the job, one of a seemingly never-ending series of chores, being completed.

These personal memories are just two of many that stand out and are typical of a way of life led in Pollokshaws, as well as other parts of Glasgow, and now long gone. In the early 1950s plans were drawn up for a complete refurbishment of Pollokshaws. The intention was to construct seventeen multi-storey blocks, but ultimately only fourteen were built. Low-rise tenements were built instead of the other three. The four flats at Birness Drive on the Shawhill were a later development. The plan also provided space for 29 shops in large and small shopping centres, a day nursery, maternity and child guidance clinics, a new police station and a library, all serving a population of around 10,000. Provision was also made for landscaping the ground around the open spaces and making a walkway along the banks of the river. By the end of the 1960s the plan was largely implemented, but it was then supplemented in 1975 by the Old Swan Project in which the block of traditional mainly red sandstone tenements on Haggs Road, Pollokshaws Road, Ellangowan Road and Mannering Road were modernised into 160 flats of various sizes. The minister of state at the Scottish Office officially opened the first eight flats in July 1975. Then in 1978 four other tenements elsewhere in the area were also reconditioned and modernised internally. Two were in Greenview Street, one was at the corner of Riverford Road and McDougall Street, and the other was the building known originally as Afton Terrace in Pollokshaws Road near 'The West'. A further redevelopment is being implemented at the time of writing, with the four tallest of the multi-storey flats being demolished with explosives. These will be replaced with a mix of local authority and private housing.

This book takes the format of a walk around old Pollokshaws, starting at Haggs Road, going up to Pollokshaws West and then to Eastwood Cemetery. From there, we move down Shawbridge Street to the Townshouse and round to the tram depot/bus garage, and then down Coustonholm Road, Pleasance Street and Greenview Street to Leckie Street and onto Pollokshaws Road. After that there is a section on the demolitions and redevelopments of the 1960s.

With the demolition of these multi-storey blocks at 12 Riverford Road and 21 Riverbank Street on 20 July 2008 another chapter in the history of Pollokshaws began. This book supplements my two previous histories, *Old Pollokshaws* (2002) and *Bygone Pollokshaws* (2004).

Seen here on Pollokshaws Road, between Leckie Street and Mannering Road, is the 25 service bound for Springburn, pictured around 1955. Coronation car No. 1204 was built at Copelawhill Works in 1938 and withdrawn in 1961. The railway bridge with the Ferodo advertisement, and Shawlands Station (opened in 1894) partly on it to the left, carries the Cathcart Circle line. At this time – before the blue Class 303 and 311 electric units were introduced – trains on the Circle were still steam operated. The horse and cart belonged to one of these itinerant individuals called rag men, who went round the streets blowing a bugle or cornet to attract attention, calling out 'any old rags'. Children pestered their mothers for something to hand over in exchange for a balloon or a cheap celluloid windmill on a stick. This photograph was taken from the top-deck rear window of a southbound tram.

Glasgow Standard tram No. 779, one of a number of designs, was built in 1900 and is preserved in the Glasgow Transport Museum at the Kelvin Hall. Seen here in the 1950s, it is approaching the stop at the Wellgreen in Pollokshaws Road while bound for Arden on the 14 service that ran between there and the university. Note the tram rails junction turning off into Greenview Street on the right. This part singe-track line linking Pollokshaws Road and Kilmarnock Road was used as access for those vehicles travelling between here and Newlands Depot and carried no public service. In the distance behind the bus is the tenement seen in the previous photograph. To the right at 1529 Pollokshaws Road is Maria Abruzzese's Maxwell Café with McNair's Pollok Bar on the corner at number 1541.

Main photograph: Behind the sleeper fence on the left is the entrance to what was at the time Glasgow, Barrhead & Neilston Railway Company's goods and mineral station. Also on the left, at the corner of Haggs Road and Maxwell Street, is the Swan Inn. Peter Swan, a coal miner living in Cowglen, who probably worked in one of the mines there around the middle of the nineteenth century, married Janet Wingate in 1847, and at a later date they moved to Pollokshaws where he set up in business as a spirit merchant. It is fair speculation to consider he may have been the originator of the name of this pub, although T.W. Crawford was obviously the proprietor by the time this photograph was taken in 1896. Nearly all the buildings visible here were cleared away around 1900 and the three-storey 'old' tenements standing here today were constructed after that date. Most of those escaped being demolished during the 1960 redevelopment by being refurbished. Perhaps the painting of a swan, seen here above the door of the inn, is the same one that was mounted in more or less the same position above the Old Swan Inn that was opened in the replacement tenement, and which could be seen there until the inn was renamed '1901' in the 1990s. The man pausing at Haggs Road has a wooden wheelbarrow of a design common until after the 1950s. He may be heading for the builder's yard on the right where the Wellgreen was later laid out. On the wall of the tenement on the right in what became Greenview Street, at first-floor level and just visible in the angle between the small stovepipe chimney and the roof ridge of the low shed, the sign for Pollok Street can be seen on a stone of the tenement wall. The two-storey tenement in the centre of the photograph survived until the 1960s and a bus shelter stands today at the gap left when it was demolished.

Inset: The white square on the wall of the Old Swan Inn in this 1950s photograph is where a plaque had been fixed which, in the days before the telephone became widespread, was used in an emergency to summon the fire brigade. In the days when phones in working class households were unknown and public telephones were few and there was no 999 emergency service, sending for the fire brigade was an adventure into the unknown. When required, there were phones that members of the public could use in post offices and certain other shops. An external sign with white letters on a blue background was displayed stating YOU MAY TELEPHONE FROM HERE, although this of course was restricted by opening times. Located in central areas of most districts of the city there were octagonal cast-iron wall plaques about two feet square and six inches deep, fixed to buildings a little above adult head-height. Painted fire engine red with a black border and sides, they had a model of a fireman's crested helmet in black on top as part of the casting. In the centre of the front face there was a four-inch square glass covered opening, inside which was visible a lever with a black knob. Beneath the opening was the legend: IN THE EVENT OF FIRE 1. BREAK GLASS 2. PULL KNOB 3. WAIT FOR FIRE BRIGADE. The plaque seen here was removed when the fire station in Brockburn Road, Pollok, was built in the 1960s, by which time domestic phones were becoming widespread.

The rear end of a car belonging to Fraser's Funeral Service is seen here parked in front of a hairdresser's shop on Greenview Street around the 1940s. Lombardi's chip shop and Lang's cobbler's shop are behind the woman pushing the pram. Note the woman in the nearest upstairs window of the lower building peering out with her hand on the sill as if ready for a 'blether'. The Commercial Bank of Scotland built the three-storey tenement with the two arches around 1900. The bank was in the nearest arch at 66 Greenview Street and solicitors Prentice & Frew were in number 64. This street was first named Cow Loan and then Pollok Street before finally becoming Greenview Street. The Townshouse can be glimpsed on the right.

Pollokshaws Road at Haggs Road, 1957. Beyond the interesting selection of poster adverts and partly hidden by the rear end of the tram is the office of J. & J. Vernal, one of three coal merchants operating from the railway goods yard behind the office at this time. The others were Aitken Thomson and Glasgow South Co-op. The flatbed lorry on the right is emerging from the goods yard empty, probably having delivered a bulky item for loading onto a railway wagon for onward transmission. The goods yard had a weigh-bridge inside the entrance; all goods transhipment yards had these for drivers to check the weight of loads on their vehicles to make sure they weren't overloaded. On the extreme right is the Old Swan Inn. The car is a 1956 Ford Consul with Lanarkshire registration number HVD 526.

The Wellgreen, 1960. The number 23 bus service was introduced during the Second World War and ran between Govan Cross and Househillwood. After the war, for a short time it was extended to Pollokshaws where the terminus was in Riverford Road. Later, it was again extended, first to the Broomielaw and then, when the city centre one-way street system was introduced, Midland Street became the terminus, where it remained until the Corporation Transport Department was privatised in the mid 1970s. Moving out from Greenview Street are two British Railways delivery and collection vehicles, the leading one of which is headed by a small Scammell three-wheel articulated power unit known as a mechanical horse, with an empty trailer that carried a container of the time. The Scammell Scarabs were early motorised goods carriers that resembled the horse and cart, hence the nickname. The two nearest trees were casualties when the first doctor's centre was built on the green.

Pollokshaws Road at Greenview Street, 1961. The bus on the number 45 route, a Daimler with an 8-foot wide body and pre-select gearbox, is bound for Rouken Glen. In the gap by the bus but set back out of sight there is a Corporation tenement dating from the early 1930s which still stands today. The Pollok Bar is on the corner and beyond the pub and behind the traffic lights on the left of the pub sign is the Maxwell Café. On the right, in Greenview Street, is Fraser's funeral parlour. The car with the 'L' plate is a Ford Anglia, a model remembered for being the first and possibly the only one designed with a rear window with a reverse slope. The half-ton Ford van has the Dunbartonshire registration BSN 327.

Wellgreen, on the left, viewed from Ashtree Road in the 1950s. Bus services to and from the city were always crowded at peak times. Because of this, a bus stop was installed in Wellgreen to serve as an outward-bound starting point for a special late afternoon peak hour service. It was provided for the large number of workers from the local manufacturing companies in East Pollokshaws such as Brown & Adam, Donaldson & Filer and Stewart & McKenzie. This author, a bus driver at that time, worked briefly on this service in the early 1960s. Seen on the corner is one of a number of prefabs that were built in Pollokshaws after the war. They were supposed to provide temporary accommodation to relieve the post-war housing shortage. Although seemingly small and garden shed-like, they were well equipped with modern fittings in bathrooms and kitchens, but were difficult to keep warm in winter. Despite being designed to last ten years, many survived for forty and, even today sixty-odd years after they were built, a few well-maintained examples still exist elsewhere. The suspended cables seen here were for streetlights and telephone cables, and are now laid underground.

Known as Craigie's Park, the field in the foreground of this panorama of Pollokshaws from 1896 is Wellgreen Court today. Could that by Mr Craigie working with a rake in the centre? The ridge with the fence in the left background, now Shawhill Park, slopes down to St Conval's Infant's School with its staircase tower and conical roof. It and St Mary's Church tower are partly hidden by the gable of a tenement with many pots that is not recorded on the 1913 OS map. It was demolished before that time and the church hall was built on the site. The Townshouse and its clock are clearly seen, but the Stag building is still to be constructed to its left. To the right, partly hidden by the tree, is the gasworks storage tank, known as a gasometer, with the chimney of its manufacturing plant to the right. The other chimney belongs to Stewart & McKenzie's engineering works in Factory Street. When filling, the gasometer tank rose up within the round girder frame. Note the counter-weights suspended by cables at the vertical supports.

Commissioned by Sir John Stirling Maxwell at a cost to him of £20,000, the Burgh Halls were opened in 1897. Known initially as the Masons Hall, it was gifted to the burgh for the use of local organisations and individuals. The architect was Dr (later Sir) Rowand Anderson. There are two halls, the larger of which can accommodate up to 1,000 and the smaller around 200, and there are five anterooms. Nearing completion in this 1896 photograph, the tower awaits installation of the clock. Note the builder's materials strewn around the entrance, and what may be workers ready to begin work installing the railings on the steps at the entrance. Opened in 1909, Sir John Maxwell School was built on the site on the left behind the halls. To the right the three short spires of Pollokshaws United Free Church can be made out, with the light-coloured Royal George building (see page 54) at the very edge. A smoking chimney behind probably belongs to the Greenholm Laundry.

The Burgh Hall, the Salvation Army hall and the Orchard Place tenement, with the remains of the orchard on the right, are captured in this photograph of Bengal Street from 1956. A van is parked at the entrance to a children's clinic, the low building behind the orchard hedge which was built as an Air Raid Precautions (ARP) post at the start of the Second World War.

Looking southeast from Pollok Avenue at Pollokshaws Road, 1961. Beyond the Standard Vanguard car is the abandoned and overgrown orchard and the Salvation Army hall. Sir John Maxwell School and the Orchard Place tenement are on the left. In the distance on the right is the rear of a tenement in Shawbridge Street owned at one time by a Jessie Lyons.

This 1961 photograph shows the home of businessman Ernest Pickwell at 2060 Pollokshaws Road. He owned the orchard and most of the land along the River Cart between Pollokshaws Road and Shawbridge Street, with a filling station and lockup garages at the far end. The front door of this house was blocked up because of the danger from increasing road traffic passing in and out of Pollok Estate. The very narrow pavement and the proximity to Pollok Avenue made it safer for him to use the back door. Pollok Avenue, now the main one-way entrance to the Burrell Collection, Pollok Park and Pollok House, was cramped with an awkward height restriction under the railway bridge caused by the arch and the proximity of the river. The bridge remains unmodified today despite modern traffic requirements. At top left is the Pollokshaws West signal box; with Pollokshaws East box above Haggs Road, the two controlled the signals and points for the main and slow lines, the main line crossovers, and entry and exit to and from the East and West goods yards. Pickwell's house was demolished in 1965.

Going by the flags, this group of friends at plot 56 of the Bankhead Allotments, which are on the west side of the railway and still in use, had their photo taken probably during a rather dull annual open day in the 1920s. Note the tower of the Burgh Hall and a couple of railway wagons on the west sidings in the background.

This early spring view in Pollok Estate from 1896 allows more detail to be visible of the stables and sawmill than would be the case in summer with the trees in full leaf. In the centre, to the left of the nearest standing figure, the exit of the sluice from the mill is visible. The slipway left of it was for moving rowing boats up and down the river past the weir. There was another slip above the weir, and the building in the right background may have been a boat shed. Until the middle of the eighteenth century there was a hamlet within sight of Pollok House on the riverbank opposite, where estate workers lived. Known as Poloctoun, over many decades it had grown and had become unsightly. The laird of the time considered it to be an eyesore and arranged for the people who lived there to be moved to Pollokshaws and Boglesbridge, which was then on the south side of the Shaw Bridge, and the buildings of Poloctoun were demolished. Only the remains of a dovecote are visible on the site today.

Sir John Stirling Maxwell, owner of Pollok Estate, with a group of family and friends in the 1930s at what was probably a birthday celebration. Identification of the location is difficult because the building seen behind does not match Pollok House, but the photograph was quite likely to have been taken elsewhere on the estate. The photograph came from Cathy White who is second from the right.

Glasgow Corporation Transport Department's Leyland and Daimler buses were predominant in the area around the time when this photograph was taken at Pollokshaws Road near Pollok Avenue in 1961. Out of frame to the left, the three-arch railway viaduct and Pollokshaws West Station were completed in October 1849.

This 1896 photograph was taken from the north end of the 'up' platform at Pollokshaws West Station. On the left side of the field, in the hedge is what looks like a 'doohut' for pigeons; above it is the building at the corner of Bengal Street and Main Street where the Maxwell Arms pub tenement was built soon after this time. The smoking factory chimney belongs to the gasworks, and the high ground to its left is Camphill at Langside. The low building, with the sign 'Lyon's Imperial Billiard Saloon', may have belonged to an ancestor of the Jessie Lyon's who owned a building behind it at the time of the 1960s redevelopment. To the right of centre, the first of the villas in Lubnaig Road/St Bride's Road at Newlands are just visible on the hill in the distance. The collection of buildings on the hill above the Shaw Bridge may be Dovehill Farm.

With Pollokshaws Road in the foreground of this photograph taken in 1956 from the access ramp to Pollokshaws West Station, the Pollok Cinema is just visible to the left, partly hidden by Compressor Services Ltd's shed roof. To the right is the factory of John McDonald (pneumatic tools) Ltd. In the centre distance the tower of St Margaret's Episcopal Church in Newlands Road can be seen, with Auldfield Parish Church in Shawbridge Street on the right. During the Second World War, some of the rubble cleared from bomb sites around the city was dumped in this field. The area to the left was where the Auldhouse Burn originally ran into the River Cart before it was diverted to flow in above the weir at Auldhouse Park.

An unusual building in the Italian style, Pollok Academy, opened in 1856, was partly financed by Sir John Maxwell. The architect was John Baird II whose partner at the time was Alexander ('Greek') Thomson. With two such eminent men involved, it is difficult to know who is responsible for what, but the gable windows are distinctly Thomson's, not placed singly as most architects would have designed them. The chimneys, ventilator gratings and the tower are more like those on his early villas. The original school was the section on the right with the clock tower. The rest of the structure, by Baird alone, was added in 1874/75 after the building became the property of Eastwood Parish School Board. The extension was skilfully linked to the older building with an arcaded corridor. The west face of the extension had the inscription *academia parochialis de poloc culturae christianae dedicata anno salutis mdccclvi* which translates as 'Parish School of culture and learning of Poloc dedicated 1856'. This photograph dates from 1896 and the school remained standing until 1968.

David Horn, headmaster of Pollok Academy in 1896.

Viewed from an upper floor of the multi-storey block of flats at 232 Shawbridge Street, the two villas at the foot of the railway embankment were demolished soon after this 1963 photograph was taken. Listed under a preservation order the 1849 buildings of Pollokshaws West Station have been refurbished in recent years. From the appearance of the playground, attendance at Pollok Academy is low, probably in anticipation of closure although it would remain for a few years while listed status was sought (ultimately unsuccessfully). Pollok Church of Scotland, also about to be demolished, is on the right, and at the very top Poloc Cricket Club house can be seen through the trees.

The River Cart is to the left of this aerial panorama from around 1962, and Pollokshaws West Railway Station, Pollok Parish Church and the Academy are all ranged along Pollokshaws Road to the lower right of the river. Afton Terrace tenement is further along the road to the right. Above the road the ground is being cleared for construction of the first of the multi-storey flats. Nether Auldhouse Road is at upper right. Other than housing at the top, little of what can be seen in this photo now exists.

In 1905 the Orange Lodges of the Thornliebank and Pollokshaws districts built this hall in what was then Barrhead Road. This became an extension of Pollokshaws Road in 1930 and the building took the address 2138 Pollokshaws Road. This photograph was taken in 1958. When the hall was to be demolished in the early 1960s for road widening, the organisation moved to the disused Unionist Rooms at the Shaw Bridge.

Looking west from the multi-storey block at 232 Shawbridge Street in 1965, Afton Terrace is at the bottom and on the left, across Pollokshaws Road, is the former hall of Eastwood Parish Church, at this time occupied by Walker's Ham Store. In the centre is the club house of Pollokshaws Bowling Club and the greens are to the right of it. In the background, at the top among the trees, the club house of Pollok Golf Club can just be made out.

With the Round Toll almost out of the frame on the left, a delivery of fuel is being made to the filling station of Pollokshaws Motors at Pollokshaws West in this photograph from the 1950s. George Davidson is reputed to have owned both this and Spiersbridge Garage and the boy is one of his sons. In the right background note the scaffy (street sweeper) in Barrhead Road with his barrow carrying a bin, brush and shovel.

In this 1961 photograph the garage on the left, built on the site of their blacksmith's forge, was the Cunninghams' Pollokshaws Motors which was taken over by Davidson in the 1950s. It occupied the northwest corner of the four-way junction of Pollokshaws Road, Barrhead Road, Kennishead Road and Cross Street. Seen where the bus is passing is the original Eastwood Parish Church hall which was vacated in 1930 when the new hall was built close to the church. At this time it was occupied by Walker's Ham Store. Everything seen here was demolished around 1965 to make way for road widening. This author, a bus driver in Newlands Garage between 1960 and 1974, may have been driving any of the vehicles seen here.

The tram turning into Cross Street in this 1950s photograph is on the number 25 service bound for Carnwadric. Behind the frontage of Pollokshaws Motors there was a large area of covered accommodation for garaging. Note the stooks of corn in the estate field on the hill behind.

The hill in the background of this view of 'The West' from around 1890, known as the Greenknowe, is not visible in any of the other similar views that look in this direction. This etching, captioned 'Low Cartcraigs - the Round Toll, Howat's House and Smiddy by James McIntyre' is taken from the booklet *The Native Returns* by Robert Watson. Born in the 1870s, he emigrated to Canada in the early 1900s where he became an author. When he returned to Pollokshaws in the early 1930s, he produced this moving, nostalgic evocation of childhood memories after visiting his old haunts. The lines on the road are cart tracks, not tramlines.

The Round Toll, pictured in the 1960s. The lower stonework has needed damp course treatment and the wall has been recently re-pointed.

On the left again is the Cunninghams' Garage, the refuelling and office part of which was built on the site of his blacksmith's forge. The original Methodist Church (built 1883) and the Jubilee tenement building are seen at the end of Shawbridge Street. Road tolls were introduced in 1750, but research to discover the date when the Round Toll house was built has been unsuccessful. Various authorities have quoted dates between then and 1800. Even Andrew McCallum, who writes with authority about much of Pollokshaws, does not mention it. When the tolls were abolished in 1883 the building was used at first by businesses, one of which was George Smith, carriage hirer. It was subsequently converted and used as a dwelling until the mid 1960s. It was restored in 1973 but now stands empty and isolated on the traffic roundabout at what has long been known locally as 'The West'.

There were three blacksmith's forges at 'The West'. Seen here in the right foreground is Low Cartcraigs, the forge and house of Bryce Howatt, at the southwest corner of Cowglen Road (now Barrhead Road) near the railway bridge. The photograph was taken in the 1890s.

Pictured at Low Cartcraigs, from the left the first two men are blacksmiths shoeing horses with their owner, Mr Curr of Merrylee Farm, standing by. Then there is Bryce Howatt, owner of the forge, with his son, also Bryce, on the back of the horse. Sadly, the son died young.

In this 1950s photograph, John Howatt is working in the field of Bangorshill Farm where Kennishead Road was realigned to join Barrhead Road in 1965. Seen through the trees in the left background is the entrance to Pollok Golf Club.

Pictured here in the 1940s, and wearing a flat cap, is another Bryce Howatt, of Bangorshill Farm. Willie McLaughlan on the left was helping him to bring in a load of hay. Bangorshill Farm was a wooden building which had been constructed around the turn of the twentieth century as Cowglen Fever Hospital, used to isolate patients suffering from highly contagious diseases such as scarlet fever and TB, known then as consumption. It stood on a small area of ground on the south side of Barrhead Road about a quarter of a mile west from the Round Toll, and was used subsequently to accommodate wounded servicemen during the First World War. For a time in the 1940s and '50s there was an individual who sold rolls from McKechnie's bakery at Eglinton Toll round the streets of Pollokshaws from a horse-and-cart van that was stabled at the farm. When farming ended in the 1960s it became a riding school operated by two women whose sign adorning the frontage read 'Zoe Newton and Melody Gay Riding Instructors'. The building survived until around 1970 and the area it occupied is still recognisable today as an overgrown plot with mature trees behind a double-leaf gate in the iron railings.

In the 1858 Ordnance Survey map this area at the junction of Boydstone and Kennishead Roads was a hamlet of a few houses known as Woodneuk. This photograph was taken in 1930 by Allan Cameron, cousin of author Robert Watson who, in his booklet *The Return of the Native*, described the house on the right as being where he lived during his early years in the 1880s and '90s. Today, only the house on the left survives and it has retained the name of Woodneuk.

The view from Cartcraigs railway bridge, 1932. A greenhouse belonging to an occupant of one of the railway houses in Barrhead Road can be seen on the left near the railway. On the skyline is the Burgh Halls tower and clock, and the chimney of the recently built steamy and baths. Closer to the camera are the roofs of High and Low Cartcraigs, the Methodist Church, and the gables of tenements in Shawbridge Street.

Originally known as Cartcraigs, this area had become Kennishead Road by the time this photograph was taken in 1956. In earlier times, running from High Shawlands and over Shawhill Road, it was part of the route used by travellers between Glasgow and Irvine; a new route to that town, via Barrhead Road, opened after 1800. At Pollokshaws Cross the old route went past the Townshouse, through Bogles Bridge and the toll, then over the Greenknowe and on past Darnley. Mrs Dean's sweetie shop is in the tenement to the right of the trees. Out of sight, beyond this building, there had been a vet's practice in the 1890s. After he left, an articulated skeleton of a pony was found abandoned on the premises. It remained there when the rest of the building was being used as dwellings and in the 1940s an enterprising local lad charged children from outwith the district a ha'penny to view it. In the centre, to the right of the Methodist Church, Shawbridge Street is seen going off into the distance. The art deco-style fluted cast-iron low-rise electric street lampposts were first introduced in the 1920s.

This view of 'The West' from the 1930s was taken from a top-floor window of the building in 13 Harriet Street, at the corner of Nether Auldhouse Road.

In this 1961 view looking down Shawbridge Street from Cross Street, the 'EWS' sign just visible low down on the tenement wall on the right dates from the Second World War. Originally in yellow with each letter highlighted with a black border, it was just one of many seen in built-up areas in towns and cities around Britain at that time. The last of these signs had faded by the late 1980s. At the height of the Blitz there were fears that the mains water supply might be insufficient to cope with the many fires likely to be caused by incendiary bombs. Bomb damage in some cases meant that sometimes no water was available. To cope with this, large tanks were built on vacant ground at strategic locations in urban areas and filled with water so that an emergency water supply (EWS) would be available. Part of the sign was an arrow pointing to where the nearest container lay. The point of the arrow can just be made out under the mullion of the double window on the corner and the tail is next to the 'E', indicating that the tank stood on the vacant lot on the left here. Usually also shown was its capacity, represented by the figures that are now almost indiscernible, again to the left of the E, in a code that would be recognised by fire fighters. The tanks themselves were oblong, with walls assembled from three-foot square pressed steel flanged sections bolted together not more than two high to form containers of various capacities. At first they were unprotected but drowning scares made a heavy wire mesh covering necessary. This happened because after a year or two, apart from the more obvious hazard of the temptation to swim in them in warm weather, not being used they became a habitat for wildlife, minnows and the like which attracted children. The sections were assembled with the three-inch deep flanges on the outside, which provided a handy ledge for adventurous youngsters to climb up on!

With the tramlines visible in the foreground this is the rear of the Jubilee building on Cross Street, 1961. The triangular brick extensions housed toilets on the half-landings which were shared by the tenants on each landing. The two youths are waiting for a tram outside the store of William Collins, plumber and electrician, access to which was at 12 Harriet Street. Note the telephone number's prefixes of the time, 'Lan' and 'Gif' indicating Langside and Giffnock automatic exchanges. Originally the exchanges were manually operated and a caller had to ask to be connected. When a handset was picked up the operator was alerted and would ask 'number please?'; they would then connect the caller manually. The automatic system was introduced after the Second World War, and new telephones became available equipped with a dial with ten numbered finger holes (0 to 9). Below each hole there were three letters of the alphabet – ABC, DEF, etc. With exchanges in most districts, when calling a four-digit number, for example at the Halfway district exchange on Paisley Road, the first three letters (HAL) were dialled then the number. A cable ran on poles above ground from all premises with a phone to the exchange, and from the early 1950s, as the system increased rapidly there was a shortage of lines. This meant the new subscribers had to share a number, which sometimes caused trouble with accusations of eavesdropping.

The number 25 tram of fleet number 41 is seen here in 1955 at Cross Street, about to turn left into Harriet Street, as it travelled between Bishopbriggs and Carnwadric via Pollokshaws. Note the junction with the rails going off to the right to a terminus in Nether Auldhouse Road that had been laid only a few years before. Up to the end of the Second World War trams turning at Pollokshaws West used a cross-over at the end of Pollokshaws Road. But as the road became busier it made this an increasingly hazardous operation, so a terminus turning point was installed here. The car behind is an Austin Somerset.

At the time of this 1961 photograph of Cross Street, looking west from Harriet Street, neighbouring the tollhouse was a Doctor Who 'Tardis', a contemporary police box, the colour of which had only recently been changed from blue to red. In the right foreground is the short northern section of Harriet Street with the old cast-iron street lighting electrical junction box complete with Glasgow Corporation Electricity Department crest. The cobbler's shop whose sign is seen in the previous photograph is in the Jubilee building with the 'SHOES (repaired)' sign above in the cutaway corner. These were the premises of tailor James McDougal who was a staunch supporter of political rebel John Maclean. The 'no through road' sign is puzzling because Harriet Street formed a 'Y' junction with Shawbridge Street, as will be seen in other photographs.

The ornate lamppost with 'Church of Scotland' etched on the glass is in front of the Eastwood Cemetery Office at 28 Harriet Street. The hours 9.30 a.m. to 5.00 p.m. on weekdays, and 9.30 to 12.30 on Saturdays are displayed on the nearest ground floor window. Note the gentleman with his pony and light trap on the left, and the coal merchant's lorry and Clydesdale horse behind with the prices displayed on elevated metal 'plates' at the rear. This author remembers prices in the 1930s to be 1/6 to 1/10 (7 and 9 pence) per hundredweight bag. The F.P. plate on the wall to the right indicates a Fire Point, a guide for firemen to help them find the mains water supply valve at the pavement edge.

There had been a laundry business at Govanhaugh near the Shaw Bridge as early as 1833, which may have been the one known in more recent times as the Greenholm Laundry. In 1891 the Wellmeadow Laundry was brought from Newton Mearns to Pollokshaws by Donald McFarlane, who had at one time been an employee at the Newlandsfield Bleach Works. McFarlane's laundry works was set back off Harriet Street (with the tram lines), seen here with Wellmeadow Road going off to the right; carpet beating and French cleaning were added later as part of the business. The works were destroyed by fire in 1902 and re-erected on the same site on a considerably extended scale, the frontage of which is seen here in this 1957 photograph. Today it is the Sunlight Laundry. Wellmeadow Road was laid out during the 1930s when the Corporation housing scheme was built. The word 'scheme' generally means a plan, but from the 1920s it was often used in Glasgow to describe new Corporation housing developments such as Pollok Housing Scheme, Househillwood Housing Scheme, etc.

In this photograph of Harriet Street from the 1950s, Wellmeadow Road goes off to the left behind the tram which is heading for Crosstobs beyond Barrhead. The number 14 service may have been the one that in the 1930s was briefly the longest tram route in Britain. Running between Milngavie and Renfrew ferry via the city centre, Thornliebank, Barrhead and Paisley, it covered 22 miles. It was a novel arrangement probably set up to gain the 'longest' title, but operating difficulties and the looming war meant it didn't last long. A favourite grandparent took this author on it for the full distance, the round trip taking four hours for a fare of tuppence ha'penny (1p) each way. Note that the city-bound track ran close to the pavement at Mrs Remocker's shop, on the left at number 74, so that no vehicles could park here for long. This track misalignment changed over to the near side of the road behind where the photograph was taken.

Harriet Street at the Auldhouse Burn Bridge, 1952. The tram on the left, bound for Bishopbriggs, is about to pass Westwood Road. The nearer one on the same service going to Rouken Glen has probably halted for the other driver to pass on information about a ticket-checking inspector awaiting him somewhere ahead. This service was also unique in that it ran to Rouken Glen then continued on from there with the service number changed to 8 bound for Millerston. On returning to Rouken Glen it continued again as a number 25 to Bishopbriggs.

This building at 11 Westwood Road was constructed in 1889 for Haythorn & Stewart, engineers and brass founders. In the 1930s, when these photographs were taken, it was occupied by the Tat Menzies & Bertoia, Terrazzo & Mosiacs Company. It was then used, in a probably rebuilt form, by the Pollokshaws Co-op Society Ltd as a bulk grocery store which was managed for a time by Jimmy Rodden, and this author worked there for brief periods after the war. Jimmy's sister Nellie was the supervisor of the society's Counting House in Christian Street, where customers' dividends on purchases were calculated. The flat bed trucks, a Morris with a Dundee registration number (right) and a Cummer (directly below), were used by the company to bring in the material and deliver the finished product.

A view from the old Auldhouse Burn Bridge, c.1900. This is the junction of Harriet Street in the foreground, Auldhouse Road on the left, Mansewood Road going up the hill past the church, and Thornliebank Road going off to the right. Eastwood Parish Church is in the background and Auldhouse Cottage and McCallum's Dairy are just out of frame on the left. The milk cart with the empty barrels will be returning to a farm farther out to be scalded in preparation for another consignment, so that the next day, after the cows are milked, it will be ready to depart before the crack of dawn. In 1906 the old narrow bridge here was removed and replaced with a wider one to carry the tramlines when they were extended to Thornliebank and beyond.

Eastwood Parish Church, seen in the 1890s. Note the two cows in the field where the new church hall was built in the 1930s.

Much altered and added to over the centuries, The Auld House in Stoneside Drive, Eastwood, is the oldest inhabited house in the parish. There is a carved inscription on a stone over the fireplace in the kitchen with the date 1631. A previous property on this site was older than Provand's Lordship Museum in High Street, Glasgow, having been referred to in papal documents as early as 1265. At that time it belonged to the monks of Paisley Abbey. Pictured here in the 1930s, by the 1960s and '70s it had become a remand home for delinquent children. In the late 1980s it was converted to private flats.

The building on the left of this view of Auldhouse Road from the 1930s is a Territorial Army hall standing on ground that was once part of Greenbank Park. The predecessor of the Territorial Army met in premises in Cogan Street, which had become unsuitable, so this hall was built around 1910. An area of ground to the west of Auldhouse Burn Bridge in Harriet Street was used as a bleach field during the eighteenth century, where the finished woven cotton was spread out to whiten in the sun when the weather was suitable.

Looking down Harriet Street to the Auldhouse Burn Bridge in 1962, after the tram tracks were lifted at the end of their 56 years of use. The gate in the railings behind where the girls are passing was the entrance to Auldhouse Cottage. Shortly before this time this author was driving a bus south and, passing into Thornliebank Road, met on the bend a low loader with a large digger. On the return journey I found there had been an accident as the digger had rolled off the platform of the loader, crossed the road and was wedged against the parapet, leaving the scores of the wheel nuts where the stone work repair can be seen here.

In this photograph from around 1950, Ria McIntosh is standing in the entrance to her house at 83 Harriet Street, above which the faded sign indicates that sometime in the past there must have been a slater and plasterer's business here.

A back court in Harriet Street, photographed in 1957 with the roofless remains of a wash house on the right. Normally, there would have been a brick compartment adjoining the wash house for the rubbish bins but here, on the left, they are standing in the open.

Around the 1920s Jessie Anderson and Jessie Cunningham, pictured here, were the owners of this hardware store at 61 Harriet Street. In the window there is a jelly pan, various pottery items, and a range of black enamelled iron cooking pots on the top shelf at the rear. There is also an indistinct and enigmatic sign advertising 'miner's oil' which may have been for their lamps. By this time all the coal pits in the district had closed, with the exception of one near Thornliebank railway station which had been opened in 1905 by the Giffnock Colliery Company. A wicker clothes basket, brushes, mop heads and poles are on display in the doorway. Hardware shops like this were always redolent of smells of cleaning materials, paraffin, pipe clay and bunches of sticks for lighting house fires. The stock also included coal shovels, cloth dusters, tins of mansion polish, washing soap, washing soda, and chloride of lime that was used to remove more persistent greasy dirt, and countless other items.

Peter Christie's chemist shop at 57 Harriet Street, pictured sometime in the 1950s. The close is number 59 and the shop beyond at number 61 is Miller Brothers' hardware store. Tenement closes then were open back and front, and the entrance had a factor's notice stuck high up at the entrance carrying a plumber's address and telephone number to be used in the event of burst pipes or flooding.

Harriet Street, looking south, c.1953. As the Redevelopment Scheme gets under way Cross Street, on the right here, will disappear, while in the foreground Nether Auldhouse Road, going off to the left, is being re-laid at a lower level. Harriet Street too is being demolished out of existence. Shawholm Street, 75 yards to the left, will also disappear in the redevelopment and the new, realigned Shawbridge Street will end there. The Thornliebank Road name will be extended to start at the roundabout at 'The West'. Hillpark Secondary School is under construction in the distance and the steeple belongs to Eastwood Parish Church.

Nether Auldhouse Road, viewed from Harriet Street in 1961. James Pollok's dairy shop at 3 Harriet Street had a cowshed at the rear and the cattle grazed in a field at Wellmeadow before construction began on the housing development. During the 1930s, at milking time they were still being brought along Harriet Street and led through a pend and along a lane to the shed. Prior to the middle of the twentieth century, before the introduction of refrigerators to working class homes, in warm weather milk would turn sour within 24 hours, so nearly all urban milk retailers delivered door-to-door in the early hours from horsedrawn or hand carts. The milk, carried in churns holding around twenty gallons, was dispensed using a scoop, long-handled and with a bent-over end for 'parking' on the lip of the churn. The scoop was like a soup tin and held a half-pint. Glass bottles were being introduced in the 1930s, but the old practice of householders having a tin with a lid and wire handle for carrying milk remained common for some time after. Most people who had a daily delivery left the empty can on their door handle the evening before. In the early morning a milk boy ran up the stairs to collect them and took them down to be filled. He returned with the full cans, hung them on the door handle and rang the bell. Pasteurisation and homogenising of milk meant that it could be kept in a fridge for up to a week. This ended the need for early morning deliveries. The nameplate on the lamppost on the left was for Shawholm Street, but after the redevelopment a realigned Shawbridge Street would end where the poster adverts are seen.

This photograph dates from around 1962, before the demolitions began in earnest. It takes in the locations of nearly all the buildings that can be seen in the photographs in this book, few of which still stand. By this time there had been some clearance south of the River Cart, but the north side had hardly been touched. To the right of where the railway line crosses Barrhead Road at lower left is the old 'West' junction of that road with Pollokshaws Road, Kennishead Road and Cross Street. The latter meets Nether Auldhouse Road and Harriet Street at the tenement with the light gable (not the one near the bottom which is at the corner of Wellmeadow Road). Old 'Shaws residents will probably be able to pick out their house.

Shawholm Street, in the foreground, at its junction with Nether Auldhouse Road, 1956. The tenement is in Harriet Street, and as can be seen, the track and two tram stops on lampposts with their wire mesh rubbish receptacles indicate that the trams were still operating to the Nether Auldhouse Road terminus at this time. Shawholm Street was a through road, but redevelopment work at the other end meant that it became a cul-de-sac, as the no through road sign on the post with black and white markings indicates. John Dalglish founded the Avenue Ironworks which specialised in manufacturing textile finishing machinery in Cogan Street in 1874. Then, in 1898/99, A. & W. Dalglish erected the West of Scotland Boiler Works off Shawholm Street near here.

The newly completed Nether Auldhouse Road, seen from a top floor rear window of the tenement at 19 Harriet Street around 1932. The area had been part of Auldhouse Park. The two men with the ladders on a barrow could be chimney sweeps or slaters on a roof repair mission.

A Homebase Store now stands on the site of this children's play park in Nether Auldhouse Road, pictured in the 1950s, with the rear of a Donaldson & Filer factory building behind. In 1927 this firm moved from Anderston Cross to larger buildings in Pollokshaws. It was registered in 1920 with the directors being Leonard Filer and Edwin J. Donaldson. It produced crimper paper cases and lace paper doilies. From 1927 onwards the business flourished. During the 1930s it started to produce hand-made cellophane bags and an adjacent factory was built. This factory probably supplied about 75% of all the corrugated paper for biscuit packing in the country. During the war the company bought the site of the Eastwood Beetling Company and made another new factory and office block to produce converted cellophane film, corrugated papers including biscuit and electric lamp containers, lace paper doilies, crimped paper cases and embossed fancy papers for confectionery packing. The factory had one of the most modern boiler houses in Scotland. Donaldson resigned from the business in 1950.

At the time this photograph was taken in the 1950s this building at the corner of Mamore Street in Auldhouse was either a garage facility for local residents or a vehicle repair business. It became a Kwik-Fit tyres warehouse before it was replaced with housing in 2006.

Looking north from the foot of Hillpark, with a recently ploughed field in the foreground of Nether Auldhouse Farm. The farm was just off the south side of Nether Auldhouse Road at the top of the rise from the Auldhouse Road crossing. The chimneys behind the trees are those of the factories in Cogan Street, probably the Victoria Pottery, Eastwood Beetling Works and Auldfield Dye Works. This and the following two photographs were taken around 1890, just before the laird of the Pollok Estate had the farm buildings refurbished and extended.

As there was probably no piped water supply to the farm, the two wooden barrels would have been placed to catch rainwater running off the roof for use in the buildings. Hillpark is behind on the left.

By the time of this 1910 photograph, building improvements including an upper-storey have made a considerable difference to the accommodation and appearance of the farmhouse.

Photographed around 1910, in the days before bottled milk became the norm, a milk delivery cart is standing in the interior court of Nether Auldhouse Farm while the horse takes a drink from the trough. Note that the man has a cash bag over his shoulder and the barrels at the rear of the cart have taps for drawing off the contents. There's a step attached to the nearer shaft for the driver to climb up to the driving seat, and is that a whip with a slightly bent handle 'parked' at the footboard? Note too the boxed-in hand-operated water pump against the wall on the right with the pumping handle on the nearside, the spout of which will be on the other side to direct the flow into the trough. In the alcove there are two baskets of coal for the kitchen stove, and a grape shovel which wasn't used for digging but for riddling the stove.

With a field of kale behind, a different milk man, Sam Muirhead, on another cart, pauses before heading south from Nether Auldhouse Farm in the early 1900s. Note the step and the thick handle for use when climbing up to the footboard, and the barrels with taps and the splash guard above the wheel. Ahead of him the farm track took a dog-leg to the left and ran off to the east between the hedges at the foot of Hillpark towards Kilmarnock Road and Merrylee. Kale was harvested and stored to feed cattle in winter.

Robert Howie of Nether Auldhouse Farm working the reaper-binder with a team of three horses around 1930. The location of this field is difficult to identify. It may be where Eastwood Housing Scheme was built in the 1950s, and the houses behind could be Wellmeadow, which was constructed in the 1920s. If so the Auldhouse Burn would be flowing along the line of the hedge.

Seen here in 1933, butcher R.J. Patterson Ltd was at 5 Harriet Street until the building was demolished around 1960. The ladies and gents hairdresser's at number 7 is advertising a style of hair dressing for women called 'shingling'.

Harriet Street in the 1950s. The occupants are, at number 1 - the Old Coach Inn; 3 - Pollok's Dairy; 5 - R. & J. Paterson Ltd, butchers; and 7 - Peter Devlin, hairdresser. Number 9 was a close listed in the compulsory purchase order of 1959 with nineteen property owners in the tenement above. There must have been another adjacent building with the same address to have that number of tenants and owner-occupiers. Number 11 was a shop occupied by Elizabeth C. Potts. In 1940 the shops beyond the butchers were occupied by McCulloch the plumber, Dunlevy's dairy and Cunningham the newsagent.

Myra Pollok, daughter of James Pollok of the dairy at 3 Harriet Street.

The shop in the low building on the left in Shawbridge Street with the faintly seen gold lettering is Galbraith's Stores. In the nineteenth century the Old Coach Inn on Harriet Street was the terminus of a twice-daily (except Sunday) coaching service between town and city. Fares were 9d inside and 6d outside, either beside the driver or at the rear in the seat known generally as 'the rumble seat' or locally as 'the basket'. Beyond the inn is George Christie's newsagent's shop and house. The car is a 1952 Ford Anglia and the photograph dates from 1961.

Shawbridge Street, 1961. Soon after this photograph was taken, these buildings, including Dr Glekin's surgery, would be no more.

Looking down Shawbridge Street from where the post box stood on the pavement at the truncated part of the Jubilee building triangle. The owner of the Jubilee Restaurant, Boni Antinori, an Italian, was interned in 1940. He returned at the end of the war but did not re-open the restaurant, although the building retained its name to the end of its existence. A property owner listed for number 332 is Angus E. Pickard, an eccentric Glasgow millionaire of the first half of the twentieth century.

Another view of Shawbridge Street from 1961, this time showing the east side with the Glen Café, known as Sandra's Café, behind the rear of the Austin Somerset car. Next to this there is a pend which led through to the rear of the building. The Mason's Arms pub is beyond the pend and Willie Shannon's fruit shop is at number 271. R. & J. Templeton's grocery store is farther on at 259. The other cars are a Sunbeam Talbot with a 1955 Glasgow registration number and, on the right, a Morris Traveller Estate with its wooden frame bodywork.

Two years have elapsed since the last photograph but here is the Morris Traveller again, this time showing its Dumfriesshire registration number TSM 574. Everything beyond the Mason's Arms pub has been demolished and a tripod is being used for drilling to check the ground in preparation for building the new police station. The other structure, a pile driver, is working on the foundations for the multi-storey flat at 232 Shawbridge Street. The tenement in the background is in Cogan Street. On the other side of the street, at the café there's an Austin A35 5cwt van. Sandrina Vetturini owned this tenement with the pub and café, and the pend between them gave access to the rear. Fishmonger Charles McClurg at one time occupied the low building on the right.

The Mason's Arms. Note the signs on the windows for BASS IN BOTTLE, a brand of stout of the time, which used to appear with a solid red triangle above it. The full advert was usually BASS IN BOTTLE & ON DRAUGHT.

Removal of the buildings which had stood where the car is parked in the centre of this view of Shawbridge Street from 1957, revealed the former Eastwood Parish Church hall, which by this time was Walker's Ham Store. The background tenement is Afton Terrace on Pollokshaws Road.

Adam Millar & Sons, plumbers and sheet metal workers owned the two blocks at 245 Shawbridge Street. The photograph dates from 1957 and traces of the fireplaces of houses of buildings that used to stand are visible on the both gables. The Pollokshaws redevelopment order of 1959 lists nine tenants of the houses above the plumber's workshop, all of which are listed under street number 245. Peter Scott, the jeweller and watchmaker next door, occupied numbers 239 and 237; to access the flats above these shops tenants had to go through the close to use outside stairs at the rear.

This 1965 photograph of Pollok Academy was taken from the rear of the Clydesdale & North of Scotland Bank building in Shawbridge Street. In the early 1950s this author worked as a junior salesman in a busy Co-op grocery store in Pollok, the takings from which were carried each Friday to this bank. Along with three or four other junior staff, we took turns individually to take it. Security was non-existent in those days and it meant carrying around £600, equivalent to about £10,000 today, wrapped in a paper bag *on the bus*!

Visible in older photographs as part of a continuous row of low buildings, the bank building is on its own in this 1963 view, awaiting closure and demolition while new temporary premises were being built in Riverbank Street at the Shaw Bridge. The bank then moved to permanent premises in Pollokshaws Shopping Arcade in the 1970s. The Afton Terrace tenement in Pollokshaws Road is visible on the left and Pollok Academy is on the right.

Shawbridge Street, 1961. At the end of the Second World War two pre-fabricated house were assembled here in the gap left of centre. Mrs Law, a popular local woman, lived in the one fronting the street for about fifteen years. The 'temporary' dwellings were intended to last for ten years and were commonly known as 'pre-fabs'. Others were constructed in Maida Street, Ashtree Road, Tracy Street and Shawholm Street, some of which will be seen in later photographs in this book. The tenement glimpsed in the background beyond the gable is the rear of a building in Cogan Street. Note Peter Scott's, watch repairer and jeweller, on the right.

The same car, an Austin A40, as featured in the previous photograph. On the left is the low building that was probably the GPO automatic telephone exchange. Beyond it is the Clachan Bar with its distinctive clock, and in the background there is another of the local landmarks that disappeared in the redevelopment, the Maida Street/Cogan Street crossing, known as Maxwell Cross. The front doorstep of Mrs Law's prefab is visible in the gap site. Occupants of one of the shops in the centre, the Doig's who sold hardware, lived on the premises at the rear in what was known as 'the back shop'.

This red sandstone building at 229 Shawbridge Street dated from around the turn of the twentieth century and was a fine single-close two-storey tenement. It was set well back from the pavement alignment of the adjacent low buildings in anticipation of a road-widening scheme that didn't materialise until the mid 1960s when everything here – including the tenement – was demolished. The close in the building had four dwellings, and Mrs Catherine Bruce's tobacconist stationer and confectioner shop and store were at 231/233. Kennedy's creamery was just a couple of hundred yards away in Cogan Street, so the delivery lorry from Pollokshields with its crates of milk in glass bottles would have been regarded as an interloper to the area. Note the SOUTH exchange phone number on its door. This photograph was taken in 1958 and still surviving at this time was Mrs Law's prefab, the roof of which and the fence of her front garden are visible behind the lorry.

The Clachan at 248 (the lounge) and 252 (the bar) Shawbridge Street, and the property at 264, were owned by Agnes Millen. At the time of this 1950s photograph, tenants of the houses above the bar were Isabella Gillies, Andrew Brady, Edmond N. Scott, James Lawson, Hans Braun and Alexander Beveridge. The low building on the left was probably the automatic telephone exchange.

Maida Street, 1962. On the left behind the temporary contractor's buildings is Pollokshaws West United Free Church with its triple spires, the right-hand of which is directly in front of the chimney of the old Greenholm Laundry. The gas lamp, one of the last survivors in the area, had a glass lifting flap in the base to allow the mantle to be lit by gas lighters who went round their district at dusk and dawn. They carried a pole with a brass attachment with a slot on the tip for turning on and off the gas tap and a tiny jet flame to light the mantle. They were also occasionally seen during the day carrying a ladder and damp cloths to clean the glass of the lights. The buildings beyond the next lamp standard seen against the sky are in Cogan Street.

Number 6 Cogan Street was demolished in the early 1950s at a time when dilapidated buildings were being demolished piecemeal.

Number 1 Cogan Street was the side or the off-sales entrance of the Railway Vaults pub in Shawbridge Street and stood opposite number 6. It was removed in the 1960s redevelopments.

Cogan Street, seen here in 1956, contained mostly manufacturing businesses including the Victoria Pottery, R. & H. Kennedy's creamery, workshops, garages, stores and a few dwellings. Shawholm Street is on the right An extract from Stratton's *Glasgow & Its Environs* from 1891 reads: 'Amongst the leading firms engaged in the processing of cloth industry in Pollokshaws was the Eastwood Beetling Co., bleachers, dyers, and finishers, with a factory at the extreme end of Cogan Street whose important undertaking we select as the subject of this brief descriptive sketch. The business is of very old standing, having been established thirty years ago as a Limited Company, from whom it was acquired by the present proprietors in 1889. The premises occupied by the firm are of considerable extent, the works covering an area of two acres, and comprising suite of offices, private rooms and lavatory, and ranges of building devoted to the several departments of the business. These include spacious bleaching, dying, and finishing works, fitted throughout with improved steam plant and machinery of the newest type requisite for perfecting the various processes of the trade. An extensive and valuable connection has been established by the firm, who number on their books the principal houses engaged in the manufacturing of textile fabric in the kingdom. About 170 hands are employed in the works under the capable supervision of the principal, who enjoys the advantage of a thoroughly technical knowledge of every branch of the works, and is thus able to give practical effect to the latest scientific improvements and developments in each department of the business. The telegraphic address of the firm is "Eastwood" Pollokshaws; and in conclusion we have to congratulate the proprietors upon their signal success in maintaining the old-established reputation of the house, and by their energetic and enterprising management extending the scope of the operations of the works to meet the necessities of their constantly expanding trade.'

This is the loading bay of the creamery in Cogan Street, with a fine line-up of vehicles built at the Albion factory at South Street, Scotstoun. As far as can be made out all have Glasgow two letter registration numbers from the early 1930s. The nearest one has the YS 7921 that originally belonged to Partick before it and the US of Govan were taken over by the City of Glasgow's vehicle registration office to be incorporated with the G series of the city's registration numbers.

The Railway Vaults pub, c.1962. To the right, the buildings on the south side of Cogan Street have been cleared away and the present-day Pollokshaws Parish Church in Shawholm Street is visible through the trees. At this time it was the Original Session Church. Note the Glasgow Corporation Education Department's Child Guidance Clinic on the left.

Looking up Shawbridge Street in 1963, from the United Free Church (the lane in the foreground runs between the church and the tenement on the left) towards Maxwell Cross. The first shop, Clyde's Grain Store at number 185, has an advertisement outside the doorway for Aladdin Pink paraffin, an odd commodity for a grain store to be selling at a time when it would normally have been available only in hardware stores and garages. Many householders had oil stoves for heating, for which they bought paraffin oil by the gallon to be transported in a can with a pouring spout and a handle. Clyde also owned this building and one in the lane behind it containing workshops at 183 Shawbridge Street (the lane was unnamed). The tenement in the centre is at the corner of Maida Street and the one behind it to the right is Afton Terrace in Pollokshaws Road. The site out of frame to the right is where the Royal George building stood.

Shawbridge Street, c.1955. Auldfield Church of Scotland is behind the lamppost on the left. It and the United Free Church on the right were separated by a tenement that housed the offices of John McDonald Ltd, manufacturers of pneumatic tools. Clyde's Grain Store is on the right with a post office out of shot next door. Note the green General Post Office Telephones Morris 5cwt van and the post box with the oval plaque on top with an arrow pointing to the office.

This 1950s photograph was taken from a third floor window of the tenement above the shops at 187 Shawbridge Street seen on the right of the previous photograph. The Royal George building on the left is in the final stage of decrepitude, with a woman brushing a carpet hung over the remains of a fence. The building was reputed to have been constructed as a hotel in the days of the stagecoaches in the first half of the nineteenth century. It is marked on the 1858 OS map, which seems to confirm the theory as that was a time when coaches were the only form of public transport, but it was probably converted to apartments before 1900. The Royal George name was thought to have derived from it being a calling point of the stagecoach service of that name between the city and Pollokshaws. This author remembers seeing the building near the end of its days when it was still occupied and in an extremely dilapidated state, but never set foot in it. Tales are recalled of squalid conditions towards the end, of leaking pipes and blocked toilets flooding passageways, and plaster falling from the walls. Beyond it is the factory of John McDonald (formerly turbine manufacturers, now pneumatic tools) Ltd. Farther away are the Shaw Bridge and the just discernable Pollok Cinema that will be seen in various stages of its life on later pages. At the bottom right is the post office pillar box.

Shawbridge Street, 1961. On the left are the complimentary engineering manufacturing companies Compressor Services Ltd and John McDonald (pneumatic tools) & Co. Ltd, both of which moved to East Kilbride during the redevelopment. Seen in the background behind the advertisement hoarding is the Pollok Cinema. Of the two church buildings here on the right, only the United Free survives. Both churches and the tenement that housed the offices of John McDonald are set back behind the low stone wall with railings and gateposts.

Pollokshaws West United Free Church, seen here in 1961, was built in 1843 on the south bank of what had been the original course of the Auldhouse Burn, which around 1800 had been diverted to add its flow to the River Cart above the weir. Before this and up to about fifty years before the church was built the burn ran past here on the side nearest the camera. Passing under King Street it ran on and went into the River Cart near what became Pollokshaws Road. At the time of the diversion, because existing industries used the burn water, the old channel had to be retained, and it became a mill lade. The church closed 1994 and was used as a carpet salesroom, but is now a children's nursery. To the right Robert Clyde's grain store is seen again, then the close at number 185 and the post office.

Shawbridge Street in the early 1930s, looking north to the Shaw Bridge from Auldfield Church.

The shopkeeper known to all as Granny Smith stands in the door of her small shop at 167 Shawbridge Street around 1950. Beatties Bread is prominently advertised in the window and Oxo on an external plate outside above and in the doorway. A Barr's mineral water poster is in the fanlight of the door.

A look inside the shop reveals an enticing display of period sweets and groceries. From the top there is Bassett's liquorice allsorts and Terry's, Fry's and Cadbury's chocolate. Inside the glass case there's Cadbury's milk flake at ½d (a halfpenny) and Smarties at 2d (two old pennies) for a tube. The shop disappeared during the redevelopment demolitions.

Shawbridge Street at the Shaw Bridge, 1956. This is the site where the meal mill was established by the laird of Pollok in the sixteenth century. Where previously there had been a ford over the river, in 1654 the first bridge was built here, and the low stone wall on the left overlooking the river that can still be seen today is probably the continuation of the original parapet. Old maps show a road going off to the right past the Orange Lodge but it doesn't appear ever to have had a name. All the occupants had King Street/Shawbridge Street addresses. The present bridge will be seen under construction in 1934 in later photographs. Founded in 1882, John McDonald & Co. manufactured water-powered turbines which were sold to various mills throughout Britain and Ireland. During the Second World War the factory repaired aircraft pneumatic equipment. McDonald's premises here at the riverside close to the bridge was originally at 1 King Street (re-addressed 131 Shawbridge Street after it was extended 1930) where the turbines were tested. Note the street nameplate on the low building between the one with the McDonald's sign and the Lodge, the former Unionist Association Rooms. The car, a Ford 8hp, has a 1940s Glasgow registration number BGE 141.

It is interesting that the upstream side of the bridge had a pavement protected by railings and a gas lamp standard with a flimsy looking bracing strip, while the other side, with no pavement, had a stone parapet with another lamp. All low-rise gas lamps of this type had a cross-bar for the lamp cleaner's ladder to lean on. The horse and rider on the bridge might be pulling a light cart with a young person on board. The Orchard Place tenement in Bengal Street on the left is seen with the tower of the Burgh Halls behind it.

In this 1896 view, at the left side of the bridge abutment there are lean-to shacks where a market gardener has stored his seeds and equipment. In the foreground, on the other side of the plank barrier, there are what looks like beetroot, carrots, leeks, potatoes and parsley visible, and no doubt there will be turnips there also, while on this side there is a good crop of dandelions. The outflow tunnel from the turbine works can be seen through the right-hand arch partly hidden by the bush. The tunnel was originally constructed as part of the system to generate power by water pressure from the weir to operate the meal mill that stood on the site. The derelict building on the extreme right looks as if it has been prepared for demolition.

The Shaw Bridge viewed from the north side in the 1920s. The meal mill was on the left where the turbine works are seen, and the building with the light-coloured gable was the miller's house. Until the 1950s it was occupied by the local Unionist Association and then the Orange Lodge, which still uses it. At the centre projecting above a roof ridge is the steeple of Eastwood Parish Church and the tall chimney of the Greenholm Laundry.

Work began on the building of the new, wider, Shaw Bridge in 1934. In the foreground the foundations are being installed and the nearest parapet of the old bridge has been removed and replaced with a wooden barrier. In the background the cinema in Shawbridge Street, then the Palladium, can be seen.

Pickwell's lockup garages in the foreground were built on the site of the vegetable patch seen on page 58. Behind on the left of this view from 1934 are the Salvation Army hall with two vents on the roof ridge and Sir John Maxwell Primary School. At bottom right a plank is visible that might be part of the new bridge builders' scaffolding, and the shadow is that of the small dwelling next to the bridge that will soon be demolished. The tenement in the right background stands in Bengal Street and can be seen on page 66.

Shawbridge Street around 1962. Beyond the entrance to Pickwell's garage in the centre, part of the old building with the roof lights accommodated a billiards hall. There are workshops and stores in Bengal Street, and the chimney of the baths in Ashtree Road, farther away than it appears here, is rising from the trees in the children's swing park. From 1967 the multi-storey building at number 124 would dominate this scene until its demolition in 2009. At the time of the photograph the Pollok Cinema had been demolished and a billboard erected on the site. After a few years a terrace of temporary shops was constructed on the corner in Riverbank Street.

Occupied by Ernest Pickwell, the ground at 130 Shawbridge Street was registered in the name of John W. Pickwell, and had two fuel pumps and up to a dozen lockup garages. Seen here in 1958, one of the Pickwells is at a petrol pump, either taking a reading of the quantity sold or checking to see if the storage tanks need topping up. The car in the foreground is probably a Sunbeam Talbot with the mascot leaping off the front of the bonnet. The one on the left is an Austin Princess and that's a Standard Vanguard being washed at the back. What's under the tarpaulin is anyone's guess, but the Pollok Cinema is again in the background.

Lillybank Place was on the north bank of the River Cart and ran from Main Street at the bridge round to Kirk Lane. This building was probably about a hundred years old at this time of this photograph from around 1900. Note the wear on the remaining stone steps at the bottom of the staircase, the rest of which, the wooden part, looks very rickety.

Another view of Lillybank Place from around 1900. A shammy (chamois) mill for treating animal skins was set up by the Tassie family here in the late seventeenth century, then John Muirhead acquired half the business in 1752. The next operation in this area was a glue-making business, which produced such an obnoxious smell that local residents petitioned to have it closed down. James Muirhead was the last member of this family which, for over 100 years, operated businesses here. In 1830 he set up the Cart Forge to make axles for railway vehicles before moving the operation closer to the railway at Crossmyloof. These businesses were on the outside of the curve of today's Riverbank Street, where there is currently a car repair workshop.

Films first came to Pollokshaws in 1910 when a show for children was started in the Burgh Halls on Saturday afternoons. In 1921 James Graham built a cinema with seating for 980 at 99–103 Main Street, near the corner of what became Riverbank Street. It was named the Maxwell for the first few years, when there were amateur stage shows as well as films, but in 1932 he leased it to J. Boe of 38 Rossendale Road who renamed it the Palladium. Boe gave up the lease and closed it in 1934. Graham reopened it and sold it to a Miss Annie M. Burns. It was then managed by a Mr Sagan who renamed it the Pollok, a name it retained until final closure in 1958 due to falling attendances caused by depopulation in advance of the redevelopment. The building was demolished in 1961/62. This author was never in it but remembers hearing tales of its reputation as a flea pit, and there were stories told of the 'thrup'ny rush', when children crowded into the matinee for three old pennies (just over one new pence). The building is still relatively well maintained here in this 1950s photograph. The car, probably belonged to Sagan. Car models at that time were known by the name of the manufacturer and their horsepower in terms of the cubic capacity of the engine cylinders. This one is a Ford 8 (hp).

This view from the Shaw Bridge was taken in 1962 after the Pollok Cinema had been demolished. A row of temporary shops is being constructed at the corner of Riverbank Street and Shawbridge Street, and later the area became a car park for the residents of the now demolished multi-storey flats at 21 Riverbank Street. On the riverside at Riverbank Street the branch of the Clydesdale Bank, displaced from 270 Shawbridge Street, was also set up in temporary premises.

Main Street, 1896. What interesting period bargains might be found in the shop on the left if the uppermost price ticket can be interpreted as 'shoes 1/11', or one shilling and eleven pence (between 9 and 10 pence decimal). Beyond the two-storey building with the billiards sign and Bengal Street, a range of low dwellings and shops can seen, of which the one with the barber's pole has a thatched roof. They would be progressively removed, initially for the Co-op building constructed around 1900. Coal merchant D. Mackie's horse and cart are passing Kirk Lane on the right. Before they were known as cafes, there is an ice cream parlour with its lamp and sign. On the near right next to Dick's footwear shop with its heavy ornate lamps is the close at number 93. Dick's sign painted on the gable is claiming they are 'cheaper than the city'. The van on the right probably belongs to Bilslands Bakers, with its claim that their bread is 'MACHINE MADE'. Note the horse dung that polluted the streets before the arrival of motor vehicles. It was a source of income for enterprising youngsters, who went round with a barrow and a shovel to scoop it up to sell it round the doors as manure for people's gardens.

Users of Pickwell's lockups, stone built with corrugated-iron roofs, must have been slightly apprehensive of the fact that the rather unstable rear walls of some of them (seen on page 59) overlooked the river from a high level. In the background, to the right of Pollok Academy clock tower is the light-coloured upper part of Pollok Parish Church, which occupied a corner of Maida Street and Pollokshaws Road. Pollokshaws West railway station is seen to the right of Compressor Services workshop, the large shed with the light-coloured roof of corrugated asbestos sheets.

The long shed in the centre, lying between the garage and the ham store on the extreme right, was occupied by John Picken's tailoring business. This and the previous photograph were taken by Nettie Wren from a window of her mother's house at 93 Shawbridge Street on Saturday, 9 September 1960.

Shawbridge Street, c.1962. All the buildings beyond Kirk Lane on the right are empty and were demolished soon after this photo was taken.

Kirk Lane, 1956. Note the long narrow granite paving slabs laid at either side of the cobbles to reduce noise from iron-wheeled horsedrawn carts when the lane had through access. To anyone nearby, the sound of these carts could be almost as penetrating as that of a riveter or boiler maker's pneumatic hammer. In the 1950s plumber Donald Sime had a workshop at number 11, and actor Alex Norton, currently starring as DCI Burke in the television series *Taggart*, lived here at number 5 with his father John Norton who was one of seven tenants of the lane at that time.

Bengal Street, seen here in 1956, was not named after the Indian state but the web of cloth produced by home loom weavers. The slatted shed probably belonged to Andrew Dickson Ltd of number 7 who may have had a joinery business, and a well-ventilated building of this type would have been used to store wood. The cars here are a Morris Oxford, a Vauxhall 10, and one of the first of a number of different models over a few years of the Ford Consul, with a February 1955 registration OGA 371. This author had motorcycle, a BSA single cylinder model B33 500cc, with the number OGA 171. They were probably registered on the same day and perhaps even during the same hour at the Registration Office in Bothwell Street.

This parade on Bengal Street in 1924 by the local Territorial Army battalion of the Argyle and Sutherland Highlanders was for the funeral of Company Sergeant Major Beattie who was killed in a tragic accident on the firing ranges. The deceased had lived in Bengal Place which is beyond the tenement with the shop with the lowered sunblind. The vehicle seen behind the procession may be carrying the coffin to the cemetery. The figure on the left in knickerbockers is Andrew McCallum, editor of the *Pollokshaws News* and author of the *History of Pollokshaws 1600–1912* published in 1925. The shop with the sunblind is a branch of Galbraith's Stores, the Co-op's main competitor in the grocery business in those days.

The funeral cortege carrying Sergeant Major Beattie's remains has marched from Pollokshaws and is seen here making its way to the lair at Eastwood New Cemetery, with Hillpark in the background.

Bengal Street on a miserable wet day in 1957. The Albion vehicle is a Galbraith's Stores delivery van with a Paisley registration number as that was where the company was based. It may have been a bread van delivering to the branch store at number 20. The Co-op tenement building is on the right with the elevated back courts at the one-storey-up level that were known as 'hi-backs', above the extended rear of the shops which were termed 'back-shops'. The building behind the lamp was originally a mission hall but at this time it was used by the Co-op grocery as a store, access to which from Shawbridge Street was through a pend. In the early days of the Scottish enclosed tenement blocks, if fire broke out at the rear the fire-fighting and rescue services could not get access with their equipment to do their job, so local authorities made it mandatory that access in the form a pend was included in the design.

Bengal Street, 1961. On the left beyond the isolated tenement with two closes, Orchard Place, there was the large, by this time overgrown, area owned by Ernest Pickwell that was known to different generations as the Orchard, or the School (Sir John's) Garden. To the left of the photographer, out of shot, is the Salvation Army hall, down the west side of which there is what was reputed to be the shortest street in Glasgow, Johnshaven Street. There were no occupants and it ran only the length of the hall and another small building, the Old Men's Hall at number 7, but the street nameplate can still be seen on the building which is now Hickory Dickory House children's nursery. Here, Crum Street goes off to the right between the railings of the Sir John Maxwell School and the Burgh Hall.

The following extract about the Sir John Maxwell School is from page 105 of McCallum's *History of Pollokshaws*: '… the school board filled Mr McNab's place by the appointment of David Horn, who taught in Pollok Academy until 1909, when he was taken back to Sir John Maxwell School, which had been re-erected [in 1907] according to the most modern ideas . . . .' The primary school is expected to close over the next few years, but there is some hope that it will escape being demolished and used sometime in the future as offices by the police and local authorities, or converted to flats. This photograph dates from the late 1960s.

Pupils of the Sir John Maxwell School, *c.*1910. The only information here is that Thomas Berney is at the right edge of the back row; he would have been eight at the time and the teacher was a Miss Kyle.

More pupils of the school, this time from 1944. *Left to right, back row*: Miss Smeaton, Anrie Hall, Kathleen Murray, Winnie Glancy, Margaret Paton, Jessie Menzies; *middle row*: ?, ?, Eva Berney; *front row*: ?, Margaret Barbour, ?, ?, ?; on the carpets: Marion Govan, ? If any reader can identify the unnamed pupils the author would appreciate the information – please contact the publisher.

Sir John Maxwell Primary School is on the left. The collapse of Orchard Place's gable wall was caused by the great storm on 15 January 1968 when the wind speed reached hurricane force. Luckily, the building was empty and due for demolition. Note the platform in the tree on the right between the low building and the Salvation Army hall which was probably built by these boys after the storm. The multi-storey flat at 124 Shawbridge Street on the right was first let in April 1967, and the tenement visible between Orchard Place and the hall was in Bengal Place. Behind the school, with a construction crane seemingly sprouting from a chimney head, one of the Birness multi-storeys is nearing completion. The multi-storey building that stood opposite where the library is today is missing from this view; it would be constructed within the next two years.

The first of the Birness multi-storey flats seen between the Burgh Hall and the school is being topped out in this 1968 view taken from the school's sports ground. The low building on the skyline next to the flats is the terrace in Parkhill Road on the Shawhill, which was originally Park Road. Below it the Pollokshaws shopping arcade is under construction. St Conval's Primary School and The Stag tenement opposite the Townshouse are visible, the latter partly obscured by a corner of the swimming baths/steamy building. Bengal Street extended to Pollokshaws Road here but it was soon to be closed off at the Salvation Army hall. Crum Street too was closed off to become part of the car park for the Burgh Halls.

The Boys' Brigade 203 Company's fiftieth anniversary celebration was held in the Burgh Halls in the 1950s and included ex-members, some of them 'gey auld'!

The public baths and steamy building on Christian Street, the boiler chimney of which is seen looming through the trees on the left, was opened in 1928. This photograph was taken in 1957; the facility was closed in the late 1990s and plans are afoot to demolish it. Before it was built there were personal washing facilities available in the form of public individual baths for six men and two women in a small building which still stands in McDougall Street.

This 1956 view is looking from the Co-op building on Shawbridge Street to the Townshouse. In the background the Townshouse tower, St Conval's Primary School and St Mary's Church can be seen. The Co-op's furniture saleroom was in the building with the Heinz advert. Above the Ford half-ton van on the right is a sign pointing to the old Campbell Library, then George Gentle's slater and plasterer's storage yard.

23a Main Street, 1925. James Munn had a good selection of sweets on display, mainly chocolates. Before the building was demolished in the 1960s, R.S. McColl occupied this shop and Andrew Cochrane Ltd's grocery store was next door at number 23.

The corner of Riverford Road and Shawbridge Street, 1963. In 1945 Hogg's bakery was at the rear of a back court drying green at the foot of Shawhill Road, access to which was through a close in a low building. In 1946 it moved to the premises here on the left at the corner of Riverford Road. Morning rolls are of course made the evening before, and this author remembers cycling regularly with a group of friends in summer from Pollok over a number of years after the war ended, first to one and then the other bakery. We stood waiting for the trays to be drawn from the oven to buy half a dozen dark and crisp, and rush home as fast as possible and eat the lot, still warm with the melting butter running through. The bakery entrance was just out of sight on the left.

A group of kids at Ashtree Road swing park in the 1930s, with the baths behind on the right. *Left to right*, *back row*: Martin Welsh (who supplied the photograph), Jackie McCue, Tom Watson, ?, ?, Willie Haughie; *front row* Andy Hamilton, Arthur Broughton, ?

Right: Greenview Street, viewed from Shawbridge Street in 1956. Two of the shops next to the pub in the Old Stag building at this time were Matthew Carmichael Ltd, chemist, and Willie Shannon's fruit and vegetable store. The close had nine houses, and the pub was at number 12 with Alfred Lyons named as proprietor in 1959.

Left: After the Townshouse was built as a base for the town council in 1803 alterations and extensions were added over the years. The low extension on the right with the roof lights may have been made into a public wash house before the baths and steamy was built in 1928. Note the woman in the foreground of this early 1920s photograph, apparently heading for the washing facilities with a loaded pram for the 'steamy'.

This 1958 photograph was taken looking southwest from an upper floor of the tenement at 18 Riverford Road. On the left is the Vennel graveyard which opened in 1770, and the large building in the left background is the Pollok Cinema. At upper extreme right the three-storey Co-op building can be glimpsed behind a smoking chimney. The gable with the adverts is on the corner of Bengal Street. To the right of the greenhouse, the rear of the Campbell Library is visible. In the RS Plant Ltd's builder's yard at 33 Shawbridge Street, the car on the left is a Ford 8 with the remarkable Glaswegian registration number AGE 868 of the late 1930s. Another later registration prefix was BUS, which the Transport Department obtained for some of theirs!

The McDougal Street *Daily Record* Chums Club, 1935. *Left to right, back row* (*starting with the girl almost out of shot on the right*): Marrion McBride, Jessie Baird, ?, ? Coghill, Margaret Watson, Eddie Burns, Jim Gillespie, Bobby Drummond, Hugh McBride, Hugh Strachan; *middle row*: ? , Margaret McLaughlin, Moira Hughes, Isabel Walker, Donald Armour, John Paton; *front row*: Willie McGraw, Alec Center, Jimmy Burns, Alisdair Armour, Joe Murray, Jackie McCaw, ? Strachan (younger brother of Hugh).

Another 1950s view from an upper rear window, this time at 28 Riverford Road, shows what looks like a mini dumper truck with two hoppers lying in the long extension of the yard of contractors RS Plant Ltd. The boys are standing on the concrete roof of the brick-built back court wash house for the adjoining closes 36 and 42, on which amazingly the curved tile vents are intact. Children in those days enjoyed the thrill of 'climbing the dykes' and these vents were vulnerable to boisterous and sometimes destructive games. The brick structure is a chimney stack with the pots missing; one from each of the two wash houses used by the tenants of the two closes. The lower section of roof on the extreme right belongs to the brick structure where the dustbins of number 36 were lodged. The one for 42 was out of sight on the left. In some tenement areas middens and wash houses were built adjacent to each other with gaps of different sizes between them, and children dared their pals as to who could tackle jumping the wider ones. Gravestones are visible in the Vennel graveyard on the other side of the railings.

Riverbank House in Riverbank Street, 1960s. Mr Munn, the caretaker of the Viking Thread Mill, lived with his wife and family in the upstairs apartments of this villa next to the mill, which was still operating when this photograph of Munn's daughter and her children was taken. The house was built by Robert Stirling Brown of the Brown & Adams Company, bleachers and finishers of cloth, the previous occupant of the site in what was then Kirk Lane. Brown was the last Provost of Pollokshaws, and Mr Munn's wife Mary, who died in 1995 at the age of 96, could recall seeing the pair of provost's lampposts on the pavement in front of the villa. When the mill closed down the factory site was taken over and part cleared by John Horn, printer and lithographer, who had moved here in the 1950s after the Pleasance Street premises were destroyed by fire. Seen here is the front of the villa which overlooked Brown & Adams' works. The back door was actually one storey higher than the front and opened directly onto Riverbank Street. The villa was demolished in the 1970s, but part of the wall fronting Riverbank Street, containing the back door, was retained at a height of about eight feet. It remained adorned with the Munn's nameplate as part of the wall until the Lidl store became established on the site in the late 1990s.

It took a little detective work to identify the location of this inundation from the River Cart which happened around 1920. At first it was thought to be in Coustonholm Road with the Cathcart Circle railway line embankment and the tenements of Grantly Gardens in the Shawlands area looming through the trees. Then the next photograph, from 1922, turned up, also showing the building with the gas lamp . . .

The tram depot is visible beyond it, revealing the location as a section of Factory Street which later became the southern section of Riverford Road. Originally it had a double dog-leg at the old bridge which was straightened and realigned with the houses in Auldhouse Road. Auldhouse Park was laid out on the right as part of the improvements connected with the building of the new Riverford Road bridge. The chestnut fence marks the alignment between the park boundary and the road today, and the pile of earth may have been a delivery of spoil to be spread out to raise the level of the park to prevent flooding. The tram depot was built in 1914 and Morrison's supermarket now stands on the site.

76

The original Baird's Bridge, built in the early eighteenth century, was demolished in 1923. Here, later that year, work on the new bridge is in progress and wooden piles on the riverbank opposite will be used to support the shuttering for it. The structure crossing the river is a temporary footbridge for construction workers and the public. The steam-powered crane would be used to haul the stones of the old bridge clear of the river to be stacked alongside it.

Riverford Road, 1923, with preparations under way for the construction of the new bridge. Using a pattern to bend them to shape, steel reinforcing rods are being worked on at the bench by three men. A finished section in a series of linked 'U's is seen standing up on the longer bench in the centre, behind which a passer-by is showing an interest. The two men on the right are carrying over another rod for shaping. The narrow-gauge railway transported materials around the site; too bad what ran on it isn't shown here!

In this view the shuttering and the reinforcing rods are being fixed in place but much work is still to be done before the concrete can be poured. The crane in the earlier photograph has now been replaced by one with a longer jib and what could be a concrete mixer is alongside it. At the lower extreme right one rail of the narrow-gauge track is seen, and the man on the extreme right might be a pipe smoker and looks as if he is rolling tobacco between his hands for a smoke.

The new bridge, known simply as Riverford Road Bridge, was completed in 1924 and is seen here the following year. This view was taken from the riverbank, from the same place as the photograph on page 77.

Riverbank Works next to the bridge specialised in the bleaching and finishing of cloth. It was founded by Robert Stirling Brown in 1893 and later became Brown & Adams Ltd. After it closed down in the 1950s the factory premises were taken over by John Horn Ltd. On the left the roof belongs to the gatehouse of Newlandsfield Industrial Park (see below) and the low building beyond is the rear of the tram depot.

The building on the right at 117 Riverford Road, a gatehouse for Newlandsfield Industrial Park, seems to stand on the site of the one with the lamp seen on page 76. It may have been a rebuild of the older one, but the only parts common to both are the two chimney stacks, each with two pots. Newlandsfield Bleach Works was one of the businesses in the park in 1913, but during the 1950s and 60s the white building on the left was a cooperage.

The gated entrance seen in the previous photograph led down to the working area of the industrial park where the cooperage is on the left. Finished barrels are visible standing on the road in the middle distance. On the right another example of the wartime EWS sign is painted on the wall with an arrow pointing to the river. The odd looking item at the top corner of the wall here is a lamp, the bracket of which has given way so that the light is hanging down and pointing up to the air. The car is an Austin A35 with the 1956 Glasgow registration number RGG 12, and Dunn's Transport Service's light truck is JGE 459 of 1951. Pollok football ground and Pollokshaws East railway station are in the background.

Auldhouse Park, c.1930. The pavilion on the right is the park keeper's office from which putting, tennis and bowling equipment was hired out. Note the number of seats for spectators and how everything is clean, tidy and well maintained. Left to right in the background are the boiler house chimney of Brown & Adams Ltd, St Conval's Infant's School tower, St Mary's Church, Stewart & McKenzie's foundry chimney, then St Conval's Primary School. The row of buildings behind the light-coloured gable at the top of the rise is in Shawhill Road near the bridge over the Cathcart Circle railway line.

John Maclean was born in 1875 at 59 King Street, Pollokshaws, of parents from the Highlands who had been forced to come south to find work. The King Street address would have been in the region of the junction with Cogan Street. His father Daniel was a potter who worked at the Victoria Pottery in Cogan Street. His mother Anne worked in the Auldfield Mill near the Pottery, and they were married at Nitshill in 1867. John Maclean became a fierce opponent of religion and alcohol and was a dedicated fighter against misery among the working class caused by overwork, oppressive employers and drink. He spent much of his free time in the Campbell Library reading up on economics and became convinced that the best way to improve the conditions of the working class was education. He trained as a teacher and worked in schools around the south side of the city, including the Industrial School set up by Sir John Maxwell in 1854. He lived for a time with his mother at Low Cartcraigs in Cowglen Road (now Barrhead Road), seen on page 21.

Maclean's main method of political agitation was to arrange factory gate meetings of workers. Curiously, after being sacked by Govan School Board in 1915 for speaking out against the First World War, he was given a post by Eastwood School Board and held day and evening classes for shop stewards. Maclean joined the Social Democratic Federation in 1903 and organised meetings in the Burgh Halls. His speeches against the war resulted in several periods of imprisonment during which he was so badly treated that it severely affected his health. As a result, he died on the 30 November 1924. These two photographs were taken on the day of his funeral, with thousands attending to form a procession that walked to Eastwood New Cemetery. James Maxton, a long time friend and fellow agitator, was one of the pallbearers and is the middle one of the three seen here, leaving with Maclean's body from his house at 42 Auldhouse Road. Maclean married Agnes Wood in 1909 and initially they lived together in Langside, where they had a daughter Nan who unveiled the memorial stone at Pollokshaws Arcade in 1973.

Newlands Depot, seen here in 1955, supplied vehicles for services 3, 8, 14, 25, and 31. Service numbers denoted the route, and route numbers were applied to the timetables followed by individual trams from the start of each day. The timing schedule was marked on a time-board given to the first driver to leave the depot on a service, and the board remained with the vehicle until it returned to the depot at the end of the duty. A curious fact was that on the trams it was the conductor who was responsible for running to time.

Newlands Depot around 1950. Tram systems were great for their time, but had serious shortcomings in that unless they ran on dedicated tracks, separated from the road used by ordinary traffic, they were unsuitable for the heavy urban traffic conditions that became common from the 1950s onwards. The major difficulty was that as the inside lanes of roads in urban areas had to be kept clear for commercial deliveries to businesses, the tracks had to be laid in the middle of the road. This meant that passengers boarding and leaving the vehicles had to walk out over the inner lane, for which a greater degree of care than normal was needed by the drivers of other vehicles attempting to pass in that lane. Another and perhaps more serious situation could occur when a tram broke down, which meant that those following were held up. In the days before mobile phones, delays could be lengthy. If the fault could not be fixed on the spot, the following tram had to push it to the next crossover and then, emptied of passengers, it towed the defective one away. Trams are being reintroduced today but to avoid some of these difficulties they are running mainly on dedicated track.

Between 1958 and 1961, as trams were withdrawn from individual services, buses took over. As they did so over the whole system, while most other transport department garages had a mix of AEC and Leyland vehicles, all the double deckers allocated to Newlands, seen here in 1959, were Daimlers fitted with Gardner engines. The single deckers used on the 32 and 40 services operating from here were Leyland Worldmaster Royal Tigers, one of which can be seen on the right within the shed here. The building had nineteen bays and had an allocation of around 120 buses. To the far left is one of the Daimler CVG6s with a 7' 6" wide body, while the one on the near right, a newer model, has an 8' wide body. Both trams and buses worked from here for about a year before the trams were withdrawn altogether in 1961.

Introduced in 1926, single-deck tram 1089 was an experimental vehicle created 'to provide a higher standard of comfort than had been the practice in the past in tramway car design'. This was to find out if such a vehicle would win back the department's traffic which had been lost to private bus operators on the interurban runs. Here, it is seen on Coustonholm Road, heading for Kilmarnock Road either during a test run in the 1950s or on a special run organised for members of the Scottish Transport Museum Society. After 1960 it was stored at Partick Depot for nearly a year, to be urgently repainted to take part in the final procession of preserved trams. This intention was abandoned, but the car is now an exhibit in the Museum of Transport.

Seen here in 1956, this tenement was built in the 1880s in Tracy Street on the Shawhill by Sir John Maxwell to house estate workers. This area is now taken by the multi-storey flats of Birness Drive In the past at one time, a few yards away on the other side of the road, there was a short street called Birness Drive that overlooked the Cathcart Circle railway line.

Pleasance Street, 1956. The lamppost at the corner of McArthur Street at the Townshouse has a sign attached pointing to the police station, which was entered from Shawhill Road (the garden hedge of the station is on the right). The council tenement on the left was built by the housing department of Glasgow Corporation in the early 1930s, and the elevated pavement on the right probably dates from when the road surface was levelled to accommodate the tramlines. If the footpath had been reconstructed at the same level as the road the cost of shoring up the gardens would have been much greater. Note the coal merchant's Albion lorry loaded with bags of coal to sell round the streets, with what looks like a 'price flag' projecting above the cab over the driver's window.

The first Roman Catholic School in Pollokshaws was set up in a building in Brewery Close off Main Street in 1829, but sufficient funds for its support were not forthcoming and it had to be abandoned. The second school was in a building on the site of where the Stag tenement was put up opposite the start of Main Street. Then, in 1857, this building, St Conval's School, was constructed on the Shawhill, on a site gifted by Sir John Maxwell. The priest occupied the ground floor, the first floor was for educational purposes, and the top floor was a chapel. After the primary school was constructed higher up the hill, this building was retained for infants until it was demolished in the 1960s. It is seen here in 1956 with St Mary's Church on the right.

Pupils of St Conval's Primary School, November 1946. *Left to right, back row*: J. Connolly, J. McGhee, A. McGhee, T. Carrigan, J. Connoly, A. Narelli, J. Niblo, J. Broadly, P. Blair; *second row*: J. McGhee, T. Fee, E. Bole, E. Hazlet, M. Harley, A. Riley, B. Morrison, M. Crawford, M. Cuthill, M. Bennet, G. Donaldson, C. Mullen, Miss McKee (teacher), T. Riley; *first row*: M. Traynor, R. Hunter, J. Mulligan, E. Rossi, A. Mullen, E. Benntly, A. Wylie, A. Cannon, J. McKenna, L. Slapicus, J. McLaughlan; *front row*: P. Harley, W. Martin. J. Ferguson, P. Mcmahone, A. McClymont, A. Farrell, N. O'Neil.

This winter view taken from St Mary's Church tower in 1958 takes in about half the locations of all the photographs in this collection. The tall buildings in the distance on the left are the tenements at the top of Shawbridge Street. Six of the buildings seen in this photograph are still standing – the Stag, the Townshouse, the baths (but not for much longer), Sir John Maxwell School, the Burgh Halls, and Pollokshaws West Station which is barely visible in the distance.

Shawhill Road, 1955. Until 1797 this road was part of the route between the city and Irvine. Continuing on through the village it went over the Greenknowe to Darnley and Barrhead as part of a long-term plan to build new roads which avoided the hills and make the gradients easier to negotiate. In that year a new road was built between what is now High Shawlands and the Round Toll along the line of Maxwell Street and Barrhead Road (now Pollokshaws Road). Around this time another more level new road was under construction connecting Pollokshaws West and Barrhead via the Hurlet which until 1930 was Cowglen Road. The lamppost on the left has a sign for the police station, the entrance to the path to which is out of frame to the left. A lane on the right near the foot of the hill, known as Dovecot, led up to St Mary's Church hall.

The premises of William Adam, plumber, at 178 Shawhill Road in the 1950s.

Greenview Street, 1961. Where the group is enjoying the sunshine on the pavement, what was then Carmichael's chemist shop was occupied by McClurg's fishmonger's until 2008, and Dougie's Dairy became Nikki's Deli in recent years. The Old Stag Pub is on the right, partly seen above the car's boot, and from what is visible of the car itself it looks like an Austin Cambridge. The cross in a circle marked on the cobbles in the foreground is of historical significance and since the tramline was first laid in the 1880s this design on the road surface has been preserved. After the line was lifted, when the road surface was redone it was replaced with a replica made of cobble stones set in the tarmac. In a *Brief History of Pollokshaws* (1980), Jack Gibson writes that it marks the site of an ancient stone cross that was moved around the time when the tramline was laid.

Greenview Street, May 2000. Efforts to trace the cross, if it was such, have been unsuccessful. One report was that it had been moved to Pollokshaws West but had subsequently disappeared. Up to 2005, in a garden in St Andrew's Drive, Pollokshields, there was a shaft on a stone base which at one time was topped with an ornamental ball. It is possible that if it was the Pollokshaws Cross, the top part may have been knocked off and was replaced with the ball during one of the moves. No mention of its origin or illustration of it has been found. Around 2005 the base and shaft were removed and a house was built on the site.

Looking north along Greenview Street around 1955, with the shadow of the Townshouse in the foreground and Shawbridge Street going off on the near left. The vehicle access in the pavement to the left of centre leads through a pend to the back of the building seen in the next photograph. The white wall in the distance with the railway goods shed rising above it is the advertising hoarding at Vernal's coal merchant's office at the railway goods yard seen on page 7.

This is the rear corner of the building with the pend at 11 Greenview Street seen in the previous photograph. There were eight houses and two business premises here entered in the list of those that would be affected by the redevelopment. The dwellings on the veranda going off to the right are above the shops in Shawbridge Street, but as access is from Greenview Street all had Greenview Street addresses.

Seen here on Greenview Street around 1954, this is one of the 46 trams purchased for £500 each from Liverpool Corporation Transport Department in 1953. In Glasgow they were known as Green Goddesses, but they had to be re-gauged to suit the track and fitted with bow current collectors to make them suitable for the Glasgow system, along with other modifications. Prior to the work being done they were stored at Newlands Depot, and even then they were restricted to certain services because others had track curves too steep for them to negotiate. After modification they were tested on the system with RESERVED showing on the screen.

The back courts of Rossendale Road, 1957. The low buildings in the centre are a wash house with its chimney, and a dustbin shed. Originally there was one of each for every close in a block. Note the wooden spar on top of the spikes in the right which, before the days of the vacuum cleaner, was used by householders to prevent damage to carpets when they were being beaten to clean them, although this short one would only have been suitable for mats. A bomb which failed to explode landed here during an air raid on the 5/6 May 1941. This view is looking east with the spire of the disused church in Leckie Street in the background.

Founded in 1763, the first church to be built in Pollokshaws was in Kirk Lane, and in 1770 the burial ground known as the Vennel was laid out on an adjacent plot. Early in the nineteenth century it became known as the Associate Church, but in 1848 the Kirk Session was criticised by the Original Secession Church presbytery for the unsatisfactory way the minutes of their meetings were being kept. In offended retaliation the church immediately severed its OSC connection and joined the Free Church of Scotland. But the members were able to remain in the Vennel building until 1871 when a new church was built, the end of which is seen here on the left in 1963, in what was then College Street (later Leckie Street). A hall was added in 1899. After the two national churches united in 1900 the congregation here became first Pollokshaws East United Free Church, then in 1929 Pollokshaws East Church of Scotland. In 1930 the congregation united with the First Pollokshaws Parish Church in Shawbridge Street and in that building they worshipped under the name Auldfield Parish Church. The two buildings here, church and manse, and the one at the Vennel which was used as a mission hall, survived until the 1960s, the church being used for a time by the Evangelical Church congregation.

Leckie Street, 1961. Not visible from this angle, tucked between Pollokshaws East Church and the building to its left was the Evangelical Church of the Christian Brethren. The stretch of washing line marks the site of a drying green which, according to this author's wife (who was born at 16 Leckie Street), was used by tenants of the closes in lower Leckie Street. Today this area is occupied by a new Greenview Evangelical Church building.

This group photograph was taken in a back court in either Maxwell Street or College Street around 1924. Many in it have old 'Shaws names such as Nicol, Boles, Waterson, Jolly, Moffat, and Darcy. Note the windows of the apartments behind where the lower panes are covered with a decorative stained glass panel or a net curtain of similar size to prevent anyone looking in.

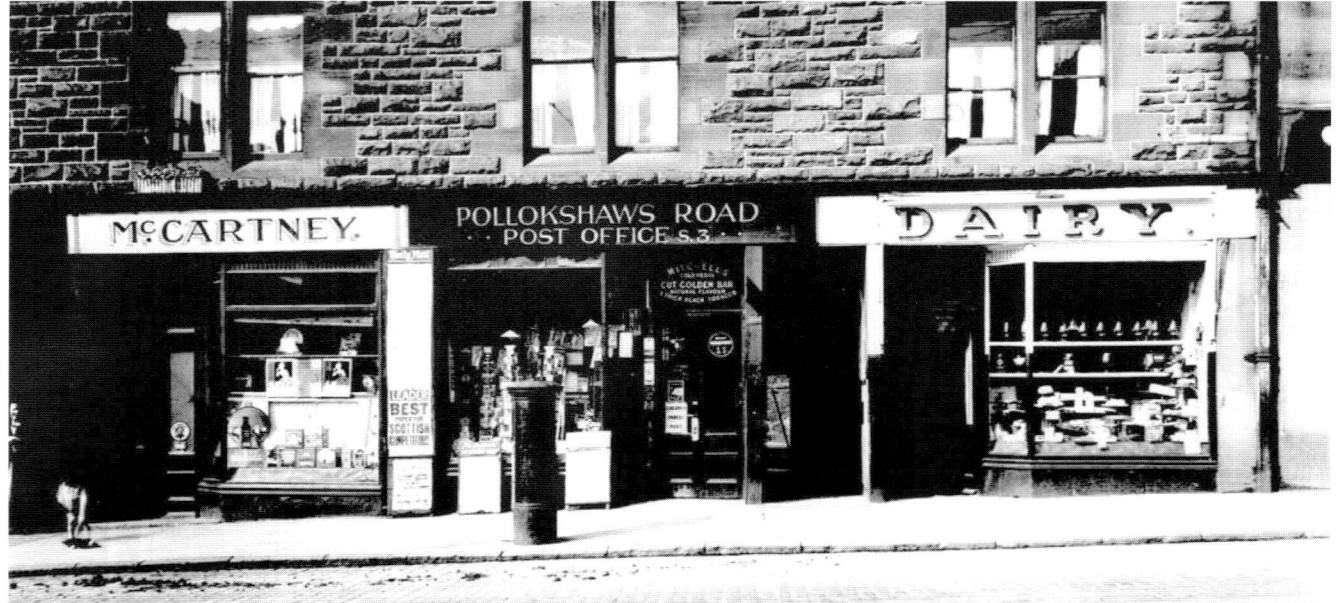

The Station Bar at 1453 Pollokshaws Road, 1931. The street nameplates for College Street and Maxwell Street have been removed in preparation for new ones to be fitted. The entrance to the off-sales counter on the left is at 2 Leckie Street.

1452–1458 Pollokshaws Road, 1935. Before postcodes were introduced progressively from 1959 (a system that can almost pinpoint each address), the one in use was much more vague in that it only designated the district. Areas south of the river had the prefixes SW, S, or SE. Govan was SW1, Cardonald and Pennilee were SW2, and the Pollok area was SW3. To the east there was S1, S2, and Pollokshaws was S3. Many street nameplates at that time had these codes attached, one or two of which can still be seen today even on newer buildings. This happened when new plates were ordered which had been copied fully from the old one! Note the advert above the post office door for Mitchell's golden cut bar and thick black tobacco for pipe smokers. The latter was made up in the form of a half-inch thick rope that arrived at the tobacconist as a coil on a small drum. The amount requested, usually an ounce, was cut off with a knife and weighed and charged for accordingly.

Pollokshaws Road, near the corner of Langside Avenue, 1928. Annaker's butcher's shop has the number 1901 but the outfitter is 1059 and A. & W. Paterson is 1063, an anomaly probably explained by the fact that while the shop was being refurbished the nameplate was replaced upside down. As a result, for a long time it was thought this photograph showed a Pollokshaws location although, of course, it is in fact in Shawlands.

Shawholm Street, seen here in 1964, disappeared during the redevelopment that decade. From the early 1930s it connected Cogan Street with Nether Auldhouse Road when the latter was constructed. The cranes seen here were for the construction of the multi-storey flats and not connected with the demolition work. This view is looking north to where, low down in the centre background, Sir John Maxwell School is visible, and on the far right beyond the tenement, is the rear of the Original Secession Church, now Pollokshaws Parish Church. The road in the right foreground was the access to John Dalglish's Avenue Ironworks, and the disappearing tenement on the left is the front of the building seen in the next photograph.

Seen from Shawbridge Street this is a rear view of the building being demolished in the previous photograph. On the extreme right is the rear corner of the Shawbridge Street building which contained the Mason's Arms pub and Sandra's Café, and which is about to meet the same fate. On the left the large brick shed was part of Dalglish's works and behind is the roof and chimneys of the Corporation red sandstone tenement in Nether Auldhouse Road. In the distance Hillpark Secondary School is under construction.

This 1964 view from Shawbridge Street looks over to the disused Pollok Academy and Pollok Parish Church. With clearance of the old buildings completed, preparations were by this time under way by Bison Contractors to begin piling for the foundation of the high flats in Shawholm Crescent and 232 Shawbridge Street.

In this 1965 view to the south from the multi-storey block at 232 Shawbridge Street, on the left is the spire of Eastwood Parish Church with the church hall below it. Farther down and nearer the centre is Auldhouse Cottage, which stood next to Auldhouse Bridge. At that time it was the residence of the director of Glasgow Corporation Parks Department, G.H. Garside. The tenements of Auldhouse Avenue stand out right of centre, and the tower block on the right at 93 Shawholm Crescent was the second to be constructed. Note the Shell petrol station and the small group of people waiting at the stop for a number 40 bus.

The view to the north from the same location in 1965, with the flats in Shawholm Crescent being topped out. At this time the *Radio Times* was printed by Carruther's at East Kilbride, for which the rolls of newsprint were delivered by a train of around a dozen tarpaulin covered hi-bar wagons and this is probably it in the goods yard in the centre of the photograph. Two days later, a train of six box vans loaded with the finished product was brought down from the printers and left in the west sidings, and later that same day the engine of the evening pick-up goods train crossed over and collected the vans to take them south via Dumfries for delivery around the country.

The block nearest to camera on the left of this 1966 photograph, 142 Shawbridge Street, was the last of these three to be built and was first let in June/July 1967. A fourth building of similar design was put up opposite the then new library two years later. That one had the height of each floor reduced by a few inches so that the actual height of the finished building matched the other three. The one partly obscured on the left, 124 Shawbridge Street, was first let in April 1967. Tombstones of the Vennel can be seen behind the Riverbank Street building on the right, with the about-to-be-demolished bungalow of the old Campbell Library seen on the left of the gap. The older buildings in the centre in Riverford Road and McDougal Street would survive the redevelopment, and behind them the Shawhill site is being made ready for construction of the four blocks to be put up there later in what became known as Birness Drive.

In the foreground of this 1965 photograph are the premises of Donaldson & Filer and John Horn, with behind Auldhouse Park, Newlands bus garage, and Riverford Road leading on to Newlands Road. The multi-storey block in the distance, seemingly under construction with the crane sprouting from above it, is the first of two at Mount Florida.